SCOTTISH RECORD SOCIETY
NEW SERIES
VOLUME 44

BORLAND'S FOWLER

AN ANNOTATED COPY OF
FOWLER'S PAISLEY AND JOHNSTONE COMMERCIAL DIRECTORY
1841-42

SCOTTISH RECORD SOCIETY

Since its foundation in 1897 the Scottish Record Society has published numerous volumes of calendars and indices of public records and private muniments relating to Scotland. A list of the Society's publications and membership forms are available on request from the Honorary Secretary or online at www.scottishrecordsociety.org.uk. The Society is a registered charity, SC032276.

Membership of the Society is open to all persons and institutions interested in its work.

President
George MacKenzie

Chairman
Dr Tristram Clarke

Secretary
Samantha Smart
c/o National Records of Scotland,
H.M. General Register House,
2 Princes Street,
Edinburgh, EH1 3YY

Treasurer
Tessa Spencer

Editor
Victoria Arrowsmith-Brown

BORLAND'S FOWLER

AN ANNOTATED COPY OF
FOWLER'S PAISLEY AND JOHNSTONE COMMERCIAL DIRECTORY
1841-42

edited by
John Malden

EDINBURGH
2019

©Scottish Record Society 2019

All rights reserved. No part of this publication may be reproduced, stored in a retrieval system or transmitted in any form by any means, electrical, mechanical or otherwise, without first seeking and obtaining the written consent of the copyright owners.

British Library Cataloguing-in Publication Data:
A catalogue record for this book is available from the British Library

ISSN 01439448
ISBN 978-0-902054-64-6

Endpapers: Plan of Paisley and its Environs from an Actual Survey by James Knox revised and corrected to the present time by Geo. Martin 20th March 1839, Crown copyright, by kind permission of the National Records of Scotland, catalogue number RHP6401

Typeset for the Scottish Record Society by Victoria Arrowsmith-Brown
Printed by 4Word Ltd, Page & Print Production

CONTENTS

Preface vii

Introduction ix

Bibliography xx

Borland's annotated Fowler 1

Appendix I 168

Appendix II 173

Index 193

1. Thirty years the Manager of the late firm of Wm Pulfer & Sons. Attempted Manufacturing since but could not get on tried a Grocery which did not succeed trying packages for a livelihood — Poor

2. Poor. Brother of Napier of Blackstown who got them the place

5. Poor — Once much property in the family now all gone

9. A good going business, but a poor Manager. His Writer says the balance sheet last week (20 Dec 1841) Capital in trade £220. Has besides the half of the Paisley Advertiser Newspaper which has, for the last ten years given him £80 annually. Can be sold for £560 — that price offered

13. Of Old Standing — Has, in Ordinary times, a good trade

23. Insolvent — Has signed Trust deed Comp[osition] apparently 7/–

24. Popular Leader at Public meetings A poor preacher

79. Reprinted in some respectable good tenanted property — No Bonds

Annotations facing page 70 of Fowler's Commercial Directory

PREFACE

The original of this volume was discovered in a secondhand bookshop in Paisley in 2016. The publication was Fowler's Directory for 1841-42, and was the 11th edition of that annual record and guide to the town of Paisley, first compiled in the late 1820s. The annotations were by an anonymous hand, as described in the Introduction. The copy is in the possession of the editor awaiting conservation prior to deposit in Renfrewshire Council Archives.

The Directory is in two parts; the main list of inhabitants and their trades, some 2,563 entries; and then lists of the various organisations and societies and their officers. The latter contains some additional information about names mentioned by the annotator, such as offices held, and this appears in Appendix II. The full directory is freely available as a searchable document through the National Library of Scotland. The current volume, in time and with material for names not discussed by the annotator, will be published as an electronic book.

Further detail, not comprehensive, has been added from various surviving monumental inscriptions in the graveyards of Paisley and from other published sources and, where the first names are unknown, reference has been made to the 1841 census. It would be a mammoth task to relate all the names in the main list to the census, and so it is left to the reader to explore individual names further.

Thanks are due to Bryan Smith and Carol Craig, Paisley Heritage Centre; Valerie Reilly; John Finlay for contributing the work on bankruptcy in the 1840s in the Introduction; Rob Close for the preparation of the index and other scrutiny; Victoria Arrowsmith-Brown, Series Editor; and to my wife Eilean for her great patience and additional research.

John Malden
2019

2 Had to retire in 1835 from a respectable Thread Concern from Manchester — Has that been kept in check by his wife Has some good property saved from the Old Concern — Old work which belongs to the family, 5 years about age.

5 Individual Partner of Brown & Nelson Does no much business for means. Highly Dangerous to be trusted individually

8 Poor Poor

9 Insolvent Composition 6/6

11 Has about £5,000 in his business, £10,000 in the Apprency in which his father, aged 84, is operating — His father had £14,000 left him 10 years ago Has two sons, the eldest of these and John in America not heard of these several years. The writer of these extracts on the bills of the parties.

15 Insolvent will have no Composition

27 Insolvent Composition 7/

28 A poor Widow brought to misery by ill doing father & son — Husband stabbed himself in his bedroom — and died instantly — Son out of the way

29 Has had, for ten years, the best trade in the line in town — Industrious and attentive and acquiring means

Annotations facing page 74 of Fowler's Commercial Directory

INTRODUCTION

The special nature of this particular copy of the Directory is that, in December 1841, an anonymous hand entered notes, usually of a financial and personal nature, to 887 entries out of 2,563, a third of the total, on interleaved blank pages. Everything about the entries suggested that someone with financial experience, a banker or an accountant, possibly with links to the Western Bank, prepared these comments for a new-comer, possibly a relative, to give guidance and advice.

In seven of the entries reference is made to 'the writer of this' and one, in particular, allows us to identify the individual. Under the entry for James Porter, merchant at 23 Glen street, is the note:

Has two sons, the subject of this and John in America not heard of these several years. The writer of this executor on the wills of the parties.

John Porter emigrated to Canada in 1821. James Porter's will survives [SC 58/42/17] in which he lists three executors – Alexander Borland, accountant in Glasgow; Robert Hendry sometime druggist in Paisley, now residing in Helensburgh and William Wilson manufacturer in Paisley. A druggist and a shawl manufacturer are unlikely candidates as the note maker. Alexander Borland, however, had been the accountant in the Western Bank in Paisley, where his son, also Alexander, was then accountant and whose son, Alexander tertius, was the clerk. It seems safe to say that Alexander senior prepared these guidance notes, in all probability for his grandson who was just starting in the business.

Paisley

Paisley has always been a place of innovation. In the 20th century, it was the first town in Scotland to have an automatic telephone exchange (1916), and it was the first town to have a Belisha pedestrian crossing of the new improved 'Pillars of Fire' variety.[1] During the eighteenth and nineteenth centuries there were innovations in manufacturing practices for thread production and weaving. The spinners and weavers were largely self-educated and well read. They were at the forefront of agitation for better working conditions and pay. Meetings and riots were quite common and, on one occasion, in 1819, the Riot Act had to be read 3 times on the same day before 9am.[2]

Benjamin Disraeli wrote later about growing industrial unrest in a town coming to the apex of its prosperity and fame, though in the mouth of a character 'more known for his zeal ... than for ... observation of character': 'go to Scotland; go to the Glasgow district; that city itself, and Paisley, and Kilmarnock — keep your eye on Paisley. I am much mistaken if there will not soon be a state of things there which alone will break up the whole concern.'[3]

By 1841 there had been a steady growth of population in the town: 1695 – 2,200; 1744 – 3,879; 1750 – 4,600; 1781 – 16,000; 1791 – 19,903; 1801 – 24,324; 1811 – 36,742; 1821 – 47,006; then a fall due to economic depression 1831 – 31,460; 1841 – 48,416.

The decade 1840 to 1850 was a particularly traumatic one for Paisley. Economic depressions seemed to occur every five years: the 1841 potato famine which caused great distress in Ireland was responsible for the influx of a large number of immigrants to Paisley, and the potato disease spread to

---

[1] "'Pillars of Fire', which are regarded as an improved type of belisha beacon are to be erected at Paisley Cross, on two island platforms used by tramcar passengers." Aberdeen Press & Journal, Sa 2.2.1935, p. 7c
[2] Scots Magazine, September 1819, p. 276ab
[3] *Endymion*, chapter 64 (1880)

Scotland in 1842, affecting the food chain;[4] there was outbreak of fever in 1847, cholera in 1849 and the general depression of 1848 when the town went bankrupt. On a more positive front, the railways came to Paisley in 1840 and the Church of Scotland underwent the Disruption in 1843. It is hardly surprising that the overall population dropped and remained static for a number of years before gradually rising with the growth of the town's prosperity. 1851 – 47,957; 1861 – 47,427; 1871 – 48,257; 1881 – 55,581; 1891 – 66,407; 1901 – 79363; 1911 – 84,455; 1921 – 84,837; 1931 – 86,441; 2019 – 77,210.

At the time of this Directory, the economic state of Paisley was dire. The Statistical Account for Paisley was written in 1837, though published in 1845. It concludes 'N.B. - since this account was written a dark cloud has come over our manufacturing prospects; but we trust that the stagnation will be only temporary'. The main industries in Paisley were concerned with the spinning and weaving of fine materials and producing the famous Paisley shawls. The recessive five year cycle of the financial wealth of the town often resulted from changes in women's fashions.[5] The years 1841 to 1843 saw the worst slump in Paisley's history, when 67 out of 112 manufacturers went bankrupt. In February 1842, 14,791 weavers and members of their dependent families were receiving relief, when 16,000 of the town's workforce, 33% of the population, were unemployed. This period has been described as the worst depression ever to have hit a British city.[6] The provost, John Henderson, stated that people coming to him to ask for relief had often had to borrow items of clothing from neighbours because they had sold their own to buy food. In fact, the Government were so worried about

---

[4] *The History of Paisley from the Roman period down to 1884*, Robert Brown, Vol II p. 221
[5] *The Paisley Pattern*, Valerie Reilly, p. 39
[6] Brown, op. cit. p. 222

the potentially explosive situation at Paisley, that the Prime Minister and Home Secretary of the time began an undercover scheme, run by a civil servant named Edward Twistelton, to help provide some relief for the townsfolk. For a Government which believed in 'laissez-faire', this was an admission that things were very bad in the town. It is estimated that in 1841 more than £50,000 was distributed to the stricken in the form of food and clothing. The town itself went bankrupt in 1842, and was not in a position to repay its debts for some thirty years.

In an effort to alleviate the suffering, Queen Victoria lent her support. Not only did she make a nationwide appeal for funds, but in 1842 she purchased seventeen shawls, and as a mark of her sympathy for Paisley, she is reputed to have worn one to the baptism of the future Edward VII.[7] However, within the Directory can be found the seeds of prosperity, where young men recently starting work eventually built up their concerns to major sources of production and wealth. These included James and Peter Coats (thread), James Clark (thread), Peter Brough (draper), William Dobie (tobacconist), Brown & Polson (starch and cornflour), James Robertson (marmalade), James Arthur (draper and founder of the House of Fraser), all of whom became household names throughout Britain by the end of the century. The wealth they generated was often ploughed back in to the town with the result of great public buildings – the Clark Town Hall; the Museum (Peter Coats) the Observatory and Memorial Church (Thomas Coats), support for education (Peter Brough) which eventually led to the formation of the

---

[7] The Sussex Advertiser, M 31.1.1842, 4a, reported that both Queen Victoria and the Duchess of Kent wore Paisley shawls to the christening of the Prince of Wales, while the same paper copied from the Glasgow Chronicle the story that Provost Henderson had been requested to send sample shawls to Windsor [British Newspaper Archive]

University of the West of Scotland, While the wealth was generated by hard work, it sometimes accrued from the most unusual events. At one stage, later in the century, J. & P. Coats were about to go bankrupt unless they increased the charge they made on each wooden cotton thread bobbin they sold. The actual increase required to break even was one twelfth of a penny. The smallest coinage in circulation was a quarter of a penny, a farthing, and this was the increase they had to charge to stay in business. The result was a huge profit.

The best contemporary description of the Town comes from the second (1847) edition of the *Topographical Dictionary* by Samuel Lewis, which is quoted in full in Appendix I.

Bankruptcy laws in the 1840s

The law of bankruptcy in Scotland was, from the seventeenth century, much influenced by statute. Merchants and bankers, as well as lawyers, had a hand in drafting and amending the bills which went before parliament. In 1839 an 'Act for regulating the Sequestration of the Estate of Bankrupts in Scotland' was passed, bringing in a significant degree of reform, and it is the system as refined by that legislation that is the subject of the present note.[8]

The law of bankruptcy was intended to deal with an insolvent debtor, that is, a debtor whose financial liabilities exceeded his assets. Against a solvent debtor, the law permitted creditors a range of legal procedures (known

---

[8] 2 and 3 Vict., c. 41 (1839). Another major statute, 6 and 7 Will. IV, c. 56 (1836), regulated *cessio bonorum* (discussed later in the text), alongside an act of sederunt dated 24 Dec. 1838: NRS, Court of Session, books of sederunt, CS1/26, fo. 300. Readers are referred to G.J. Bell, *Principles of the Law of Scotland* (4th edn, Edinburgh, 1839), for more detail

collectively as 'diligence') which permitted them to seize or freeze assets owned by the debtor. For instance, by means of arrestment a debtor could arrest a fund owed to his debtor that was in the hands of a third party, attaching the debt until his own debt was paid. The ancillary action of forthcoming (pronounced 'furthcoming') was the means by which the creditor could obtain by court order as much of the arrested fund as required to cover the debt and his expenses. Another type of diligence was the inhibition. By means of an inhibition executed against him, and registered in the register of inhibitions, a debtor could be ordered not to alienate his heritable property or otherwise to deal with it in a way prejudicial to the inhibiter. By an action of adjudication the land could then be transferred to the creditor who would possess it, and draw income from it, until the debt was satisfied. Diligence of this kind might be in execution of a court decree against the debtor or it might be in security. A further type of diligence was imprisonment of the debtor. This followed a warrant requiring the debtor to pay or to face poinding (seizure of his moveable goods) or imprisonment, such warrant being obtained from the Court of Session (routinely in the extract obtained by the creditor of a court degree) or, from 1839, from the sheriff court.[9]

A debtor could face bankruptcy in a variety of trading situations but also personal relationships could lead to difficulties. A number of law agents, for example, became insolvent as a result of guaranteeing a debt for client which the client could not subsequently repay. In trade, various mechanism for giving credit might be used. There is reference in one of the entries, for example, to an 'Accommodation', a reference to an accommodation bill.[10]

---

[9] This was regulated by an act of sederunt dated 6 Jun. 1839: NRS, Court of Session, sederunt books, CS1/27 fo. 3
[10] See entry no.14 on Fowler page 14, and elsewhere

This was a bill of exchange granted by A (the drawee) to B (the drawer) based on no underlying transaction, often done to assist a friend. This facilitated B in gaining credit for the amount in the bill. A would accept the bill and B would sell it to C (for instance, a bank) at a discount. By the time the bill matured and became payable, the intention was that B would have paid the value of the bill to A who could then honour it. In the event that B was unable to pay, A remained liable for the debt. This type of bill, known sometimes as a 'Wind Bill' in Scotland because the underlying debt was fictitious—it was 'a mere accommodation'—had several varieties but the drawee and acceptor always took the risk that B would be able to pay what was required to honour the bill.[11]

Sequestration of an insolvent debtor was tightly regulated in the 1839 Act. It could proceed with or without the debtor's consent. If without, the debtor was required to appear in the Court of Session to explain why sequestration should not proceed. Even with consent, only one or more 'qualifying creditors' could seek sequestration, that is, creditors owed above a prescribed sum, and they had to take an oath of verity and provide documentary evidence as to the existence of the debt.

Where a debtor operated in a commercial context (such as merchant, tradesman, banker) or was a company, and was thought to be insolvent, his creditors could apply to the Court of Session for the sequestration of his estate under an Act of 1696.[12] The debtor himself could also apply for sequestration.[13] If the petition for sequestration was without the debtor's consent, he was cited to appear before the lord ordinary to show cause why it should not proceed. If he failed

---

[11] Bell, *Principles*, 346

[12] *Records of the Parliament of Scotland* [*RPS*], ed. K.M. Brown et al., (St Andrews, 2007-2014), 1696/9/57; 2 and 3 Vict. c. 41, ss. 5, 6

[13] 2 and 3 Vict. c. 41, s. 13

to appear or to show cause, the judge could award sequestration provided there was sufficient evidence of notour bankruptcy (on which, see below). From 1839, once the lord ordinary in the Court of Session awarded sequestration, the remaining procedure was remitted to the sheriff court subject to the requirement that the lord ordinary appoint a meeting of the creditors to be held within a fortnight to elect an interim factor, and a further meeting to be held within six weeks to elect a trustee (or trustees) and commissioners.[14]

The role of the trustee and three commissioners elected by the creditors was to sell and distribute the estate amongst the entire body of creditors. As soon as the trustee in bankruptcy was confirmed by the court, the debtor's estate vested in him and he was empowered to deal with the heritable and moveable property of the bankrupt; to ingather debts owing to him and to establish, through examination of accounts and vouchers, who was owed what (subject to review by a judge in the event of dispute). A list of the creditors entitled to draw a dividend had to be drawn up and the creditors notified.[15]

The policy of the law was equitable: it sought to ensure equality amongst unsecured creditors (that is, creditors who had secured no preference in the debtor's estate through, for example, a heritable security in land belonging to him). The law also sought to free the debtor, eventually, from the burden of his debt by providing him with the right to apply for a discharge provided the majority of his creditors consented and the sheriff saw fit to grant it.

An insolvent person became known as a 'notour bankrupt' in certain circumstances following on a court ordering him to pay a debt, either by failing to pay, having an action of

---

[14] Ibid. Precise time limits were set in the legislation
[15] Ibid., ss. 104, 105

sequestration brought against him, or, for example, avoiding making payment by fleeing the country or entering a debtors' sanctuary.[16] At that point, the law imposed rules on how the debtor could deal with his property. He could not give it away, or sell it cheaply, to his friends and relations because this would deny his creditors the opportunity to sell it at market price in order to recover what was owed. This rule against 'gratuitous alienations' of property imposed a presumption that such transactions were fraudulent and null.[17]

Likewise, it was unlawful to favour one creditor over another by granting them a preference just prior to bankruptcy. Secured creditors were preferred (i.e. paid prior) to unsecured creditors and secured creditors generally ranked by the date of their security according to the principle prior tempore potior jure ('earlier by time, stronger by right'). Unsecured creditors, on the other hand, would normally all seek payment of their debt simultaneously in the event of insolvency when, of course, the debtor was by definition not in a position to satisfy all debts in full. Therefore, the law sought to equalise these creditors (the technical term used was ranking pari passu i.e. they ranked on an equal footing). Creditors who arrested or poinded the debtor's moveable property within sixty days prior to his bankruptcy, or four months thereafter, ranked as though they had exercised this diligence at the same date.[18] What creditors could expect in

---

[16] *RPS*, 1696/6/57

[17] Ibid., 1621/6/30

[18] Arrestment, as noted, referred to the attachment of a fund or moveable item which was owned or possessed by a third party but legally due to the debtor. A debt of money owed to the debtor, for instance, had to be arrested. Poinding was the attachment of corporeal moveable property owned by the debtor (poinding of the ground was also possible but was procedurally different). The property could be in the possession of the debtor or in the custody

such circumstances was payment of a percentage of the sum owed, depending on the assets remaining in the debtor's estate (once secured creditors, of course, had been satisfied).

The process of cessio bonorum (surrender of goods), derived from Roman law, was a means of allowing the debtor to apply for protection. The sheriff would question the bankrupt and his creditors and investigate his affairs in order to discover the full extent of his estate. Decree of cessio gave the creditors full right to the moveable estate of the bankrupt and obliged him to convey his heritable property to them. For the debtor, however, it meant liberation from prison.

The process of sequestration came to an end normally when the bankrupt was discharged. The debtor applied for discharge to the sheriff as soon as he had the agreement of all of his creditors or, with the consent of a majority of them (representing at least four-fifths of the value of the debt), he could apply eight months after the award of sequestration was made. The sheriff then had to decide whether to grant discharge or to do so subject to conditions. Alternatively, the debtor might offer to pay a composition. This was a sum which the majority of creditors (provided they represented nine-tenths in value of the debts owed), at a meeting called for the purpose, were willing to accept from the debtor in satisfaction of all his debts.[19] If the creditors agreed to a composition, and the debtor was able to find a cautioner (guarantor) in respect of it, then he was discharged from bankruptcy. In any case of discharge, the debtor had to swear that he had made a full and fair surrender of his estate.

Two aspects of bankruptcy processes should be stressed. First, legal procedure was tightly regulated. For instance,

---

of a third party and there were some exceptions to the kind of item that could be poinded.

[19] 2 and 3 Vict. c. 51, s. 114

debtors had to be judicially examined as to the extent of their estates, and at least one creditor had to give an oath and prove their debts in court before sequestration could be awarded. Secondly, part of the procedure was intended to ensure publicity. All creditors were entitled to know what was happening so that they could protect their interests. This led to requirements, at various stages, for public advertisements in the *Edinburgh Gazette* and notice to be given to creditors that proceedings were underway.[20]

---

[20] 6 and 7 Will. IV, c. 56, s. 4

SELECTED BIBLIOGRAPHY

Historical Description of the Abbey and Town of Paisley, Charles Mackie, Swan, Glasgow, 1835

A Topographical Dictionary of Scotland, Samuel Lewis, S. Lewis, London, 2nd edition 1847

The History of the Paisley Grammar School, Robert Brown, Alexander Gardner, 1875

History of the High Church, Paisley, Robert Brown, Alexander Gardner, Paisley, 1878

The History of Paisley from the Roman period down to 1884, Robert Brown, J. & J. Cook, Paisley, 1886

Peter Brough, a Paisley philanthropist, James B. Sturrock, Alexander Gardner, Paisley, 1890

Paisley Weavers of Other Days, David Gilmour, David Douglas, Edinburgh, 1898

The Paisley Thread Industry and the Men who Created and Developed it, Matthew Blair, Alexander Gardner, Paisley, 1907

A History of Paisley, 600-1908, W.M. Metcalfe, Alexander Gardner, Paisley, 1909

Glasgow and Paisley Eighty Years Ago, John Urie, Alexander Gardner, Paisley, 1910

The Story of Paisley, C. Stewart Black, J. & J. Cook, Paisley, 1948

A Social Geography of Paisley, Mary McCarthy, Paisley Public Library, Paisley, 1969

John Henning 1771-1851 "a very ingenious Modeller", John Malden, Renfrew District Council, Paisley, 1977

The Paisley Pattern: the Official Illustrated History, Valerie Reilly, Richard Drew, Glasgow, 1987

Paisley: A History, Sylvia Clark, Mainstream, Edinburgh, 1988

A Legend in Retailing... House of Fraser, Michael Moss and Alison Turton, Weidenfeld & Nicholson, London, 1989

Golden Threads: A Look at Paisley's Past, David Rowand, Paisley Daily Express, Paisley, 1999

The Monastery & Abbey of Paisley, John Malden, Renfrewshire Local History Forum, Paisley, 2000

Schools in Paisley before 1872, William J. McKechin, Renfrewshire Local History Forum, Paisley, 2000

Silver Threads: A Look at Paisley's Past, David Rowand, Paslet Publications, Paisley, 2000

David Rowand's Paisley, David Rowand, Paslet Publications, Paisley, 2001

Seams Sewn Long Ago: the Story of Coats the Threadmakers, Brian Coats, CreateSpace Independent Publishing Platform, 2013

The Brewers and Breweries of Ayrshire, Buteshire and Renfrewshire, Forbes Gibb and Rob Close, Lomax Press, Stirling, 2013

Woodside Cemetery Paisley: Memorial Inscriptions and Garden of Remembrance, Renfrewshire Family History Society (compact disk), Gourock

The Paisley & Renfrewshire Gazette

The Royal Military Chronicle, Vol.6, May 1813

Scotch Reformers' Gazette 1837-48, later (1849-54) *Reformers' Gazette* and (1854) *Glasgow Gazette*

The Edinburgh Gazette

The Paisley Magazine, nos. I-XIII, ed. William Motherwell, David Dick, Paisley, 1828

The Statistical Account of Renfrewshire, Vol VII, Burns, Macnair et al., William Blackwood, Edinburgh, 1845

BORLAND'S ANNOTATED FOWLER

Editorial conventions

The original notated entries, which are on Fowler's Directory pages 13 to 95, were given a line number by Alexander Borland and this number related to his notes written on the facing page. In this transcription, entry lines in bold in the transcribed pages indicate Borland's entry on the facing page. Round ( ) brackets around entry lines are where Borland has omitted a reference number but made a comment, often in the margin. Where Borland has miscounted the lines, i.e. on pp. 15, 59, 60, 64, 66, 69 and 92, or has (p. 35) numbered his remarks consecutively, his numbering has been retained. Square brackets [ ] are editorial interpolations, with question marks for uncertain readings. Footnotes are numbered a, b, c.

Additional information about an individual is given in Appendix II using Arabic numbered references. This information has been drawn from the 1841 Census, especially the ages of individuals; other sections of Fowler's Paisley and Johnstone Commercial Directory for 1841-42; earlier Fowler's Directories for 1829, 1835, 1838; Dick & Macgregor's Directory of 1840; the *Paisley & Renfrewshire Gazette*; monumental inscriptions; and other sources, as noted in the bibliography.

FOWLER'S PAISLEY DIRECTORY.

ABBEY CHURCH, 16 Smithhills, and 7 Abbey Close—was erected in 1160, during the reign of Malcolm IV., by Walter, Lord High Steward of Scotland; strangers, or others wishing admittance, may apply to Thomas Ewing, officer, 29 New Smithhills

Abbey Sounding Aisle, 9 Abbey Close—John M'Donald, key-keeper, 6 Abbey Street

Abercrombie, William, harbour-master and collector of river dues—house Swing Bridge, River Cart

Adam, Alexander, boot and shoemaker, 148 George street

Adam, Alexander, gardener, 2 Old Sneddon street

Adam George, chimney sweep, vent mender and curer, 6 Lawn street

Adam, J. & J., feuars and farmers—house 10 Neilston street, and quarriers, Wilkins Quarry

Adam, James, feuar, Carriagehill

Adam, James, window glazier, 2 Lillias' Wynd, ho. 1 do.

Adam, Janet, cowfeeder, 13 Orchard street

Adam, John, clerk, Glasgow Union Bank, 109 High street —house 11 Smithhills

Adam, John, of Collinslee, residence, Helensburgh

Adam, John, flesher, 17 Smithhills

Adam, John, pattern drawer, 9 Shuttle street

Adam, John, watch and clock maker, 11 Smithhills

Adam, Matthew—house 10 Neilston street

Adam, Miss Mary, grocer, 9 Moncrieff street

Adam, Misses, crape dressers, and straw hat makers, 11 Smithhills

Adam, Peter, vintner, and keeper of bowling green, 37 Oakshaw street

Adam, Robt., cutler and edge tool maker, 14 St. Mirren st.

Entry	**Page 13**
3	*Without means – a precarious living*
7[1]	*Now easy in circumstances back as farmers feuars and quarriers. In 1837 a Brother committed suicide involving £3,200 of which they have only got 10/- which has much embarrassed them. Other 3/- per £ is expected*
9	*Well doing Man but very limited in means. Poor*
11	*Absconded taking in both Bank & many friends*
12[2]	*Considerable annuity from his Father in law the late Wm King but requires it all and more. The Family wealthy but extravagant & expensive they have the property in fee. Collinslee the father's property, burthened £4,500 to the Trustees*
13	*Has fair trade but small means. Is indebted to his Aunt Mrs McKay who guarantees his Cr a/c*
(15)	*Poor*
(16)[3]	*Ditto*
19[4]	*Totally without means*
20[5]	*A journeyman newly commenced. No means*

Adam, Robt., flesher, 36 High street—ho. 9 Orr square
Adam, Robt., manager of thread work, 70 New Sneddon st.
Adam, Robert, spirit dealer, 49 Moss street—house 12 Dyer's Wynd
Adam, Thomas, 86 High street
Addison, Mrs., dressmaker, 69 High street
Addison, William & Co., shawl merchants, 6 Cumberland Court, 110 Causeyside
Addison, Wm., of Addison Wm. & Co.—ho. 69 High st.
Advertiser Office, (Paisley,) 15 St. Mirren street, published on Saturday morning at 7 o'clock
Agnew, Robt , grocer, cabinet and chair maker, agent for Morrison's vegetable universal medicine, 69 High st.
Agnew, William, blacksmith, 93 High street—house do.
Aikman, Edward, clothlapper, Cumberland place—house Camphill
Aitken, James, cowfeeder, 61 George street
Aitken, James, late chandler, 1 Water brae (burgh)
Aitken, Mat., spirit dealer (carriers' quarters) 12 Causeyside
Aitken, Robert, cartwright, 62 George street
Aitken, William, joiner and cartwright, 89 George street
Aitken, William, stationer and newsman, 81 High street, and teacher, 35 Castle street—house 12 do.
Alexander, James, shoemaker, 67 High street
Alexander, John, pattern drawer, 5 Causeyside—house 74 Love street
Alexander, Miss A., dressmaker, 67 High street
Alexander, Mrs. William, dressmaker, 20 Inkle street
Alexander, Robert, tailor, 37 Stock street
Alexander, Walter, flesher, 107 George street
Alexander, William, weaver's wright, 8 Stock street
Algie, John, farmer, Corker hill
Allan, David, boot and shoemaker, 31 High street
Allan, John, sheriff officer and constable for Renfrewshire and Lanarkshire, 70 Stockwell street, Glasgow
Allan, Mrs., teacher, 21 High street
Allison, David, precentor North Church—house 12 New Sneddon
Allison, John, ginger-beer manufacturer, spirit dealer and ale bottler, 31 Caledonia street

Entry	**Page 14**
1	*Father of John Adam, flesher, above. Left the son in anger. Has no means, nor much business*
3	*Has been 12 or 15 years in the same shop. Has a good business with the very lowest of characters. The soubriquet of Shop Bugle Hall*
5, 6	*Succeeded Andrew Barclay at May last in this line of business. Had about £200 and a property, which, 2 years ago gave £600 for. A cautious careful family. No children. Partner unknown, supposed to be none*
8	*Shared by Robt Hay Editor & John Neilson printer. Pays well & is increasing*
11	*Failed 1827. Afterwards paid up his debts. Failed again 1841 paid 5/-*
12[1]	*Had some property, but is now poor*
13[2]	*Wealthy – out of all business*
14	*Came to Paisley from Kilbarchan, with some means. Has this year 1841 been taken in by Accommodation[a] and though not failed is very poor*
15	*Brother of James, cowfeeder, above in same circumstances*
16	*Ditto*
17[3]	*As poor as Lazerous*
25	*Respectable and supposed to have means*
30	*Has been 10 years in the line but is not supposed to have done any good. Always scarce of money. 1842 January Rouped out*

---

[a] See discussion in the Introduction, p. xiii

Allison, Mrs., spirit dealer, 8 School wynd
Allison, Walter, timber merchant, 69 Broomlands—house 3 William street
Anderson, Ebenezer, 2 Moss street
Anderson, James, bird stuffer, 18 Lawn street
Anderson, James & Co., funeral undertakers, 39 New st.
Anderson, James, leather cutter and shoemaker, 40 Well-meadow
Anderson, James, grocer and spirit dealer, 75 Love street
Anderson, James, of Glen, Anderson & Co.—ho. Blackhall
Anderson, James, salesman, coal yard, Harbour Lane—house 27 Back Sneddon
Anderson, James, teacher, 7 South Croft street
Anderson, John, grocer and spirit dealer, 71 Love street
Anderson, John, printer at Baird and Wallace's—house 5 Caledonia street
Anderson, John, of Anderson and Semple, and procurator fiscal for the burgh, Gilmour street—house do.
Anderson, Mrs., grocer and spirit dealer, Carriagehill
Anderson, Mrs., milliner and dressmaker, 44 Moss street
Anderson, Mrs., milliner and dressmaker, 16 Newton street
Anderson, Robert, cowfeeder, 3 Prussia street
Anderson, Robert, Saracen's Head Inn, 2 Moss street—job and post horses, coaches, noddies, and gigs, hearses, mourning coaches, &c.
Anderson and Semple, writers, Gilmour street
Anderson, Thomas, Washington Inn, 78 High street
Anderson, William, bookseller, 41 Wellmeadow
Anderson, William, thibet cropper and shawl cutter, 10 Bridge street (burgh)—house 13 George street
Andrew, Henry, spirit dealer, 32 George street
Andrew, John, bookseller and librarian, 19 Lawn street
Andrew, John, lead drawer, 19 Lawn street
Andrew, Thomas, grocer, Carriagehill
Angus, J., straw hat maker, 2 Love street
Armour, Robert, grocer and spirit dealer, 1 George street
Armour, Robert, cooper, grocer and ham curer, 8 Church hill—cooperage, 7 do.
Arneil, William, joiner, cartwright, and smith, 3 Burn row, and 12 Bridge street (burgh)

Entry	**Page 15**
1	*A poor widow struggling with the world*
2	*Wealthy – has considerable means in property and in houses both in Paisley & Greenock and shares in several vessels*
5	*No means*
7	*Is supposed to have considerable means, has a good business of longstanding and much good paying property*
11	*Has a good business attended by all the <u>laighland</u> farmers, though not wealthy is in good credit and some means*
13[1]	*Complete miser. Has acquired considerable property*
18	*Bankrupt owing £1,800 supp composition 10/-*
20	*A rough going gambling house. Not wealthy but has for 10 years always paid his way*
21[2]	*Oct 1841 Dead, has left from £300 to £400*
27[3]	*Has considerable property left by his father who died last year*
28[4]	*Was put into trade and supported by Mr King his brother in law about 10 years ago. Is doing well*
29	*A long established trader. Has a little property and cautious – July 1842 dead*

PAISLEY.

Arthur, Arch., of Arthur, Arch. & Co.—ho. 8 West Croft st.
Arthur, Arch. & Co. shawl manufacturers, 8 Causeyside
Arthur, James, draper and hosier, 18 High street
Arthur, Matthew, of Robertson, Matthew & Co.—house Causey-end
Ashworth, John, carding master, Adelphi mill, 68 New Sneddon
Auld, Alexander, agent, 15 Causeyside—house Wellington Cottage, 7 Stow place
Auld, John, sub-distributor of stamps, and sub-collector of assessed taxes, 3 Christie terrace—ho. 62 Love street
Auld, Misses, milliners and dressmakers, 95 High street
Ayton, David, gas inspector—house 28 Lady lane

BAILEY, Robert, wine and spirit merchant, 14 Old Sneddon, and 97 New Sneddon—house 96 do.
Bailey, David, grocer and spirit dealer, 23 Williamsburgh
Baillie, William, at Lyall, William & Sons, 90 High street—house 32 Glen street
Bain, James, baker, 144 George street
Bain, John, jun., moulder and musician, 35 High street
Bain, John, teacher of dancing, 3 St. James' street
Bain, Miss,—house 24 Orchard street
Bain, William, ironmonger, 109 High street—ho. 92 do.
Baird, Charles, manufacturer, 43 George street
Baird, James, farmer, Whitehaugh
Baird, James, grocer and cowfeeder, 19 New Smithhills
Baird, John, of Baird & Wallace—house 46 Love street
Baird, John, jun., manager, printworks, Nethercommon,—house 59 Love street
Baird, John, traveller for Harvey, Jas. & Co.—house 23 Causeyside
Baird, Miss, matron, Town Hospital, 7 New Sneddon
Baird, Misses, milliners and dress makers, 31 High street
Baird, Misses, milliners, straw hat & dress makers, 27 George street
Baird, Mrs. George, farmer, Oldhall
Baird, Rev. Archibald, U. S. C. house, 57 Love street
Baird & Wallace, manufacturers, 9 and 10 Forbes' place—calico and shawl printers, Nethercommon

Entry	**Page 16**
1[1]-2	*Has been in business about 8 years. Has never done much, nor in good credit. Has no means. March 1842 Bankrupt*
3	*Bought a bankrupt stock when he commenced business in 1836, paid £800 cash for it. Was at that time a stranger. Is well behaved and said to be well connected. The father considerable means & in no trade*
4[2]	*Father of the above. Bleachfield Manager*
6	*Failed in 1839. Has not got on since. Has no means*
7[3]	*Lives above his income at all times. Always hard up. To be avoided in cash matters though gentlemanly and respected in society 1842 February £800 balance & expelled*
10	*Dead. Bankrupt*
11	*In good repute and has some property*
12	*Has commenced on his own account at 18 Causeyside. Has no means, but from his careful good behaviour has got into credit. Is the son of a most disreputable father but whose family are all well doing*
13[4]	*Has no means of his own – but has succeeded to his father's trade who has retired to live on his means – very wealthy – His father must have gifted him a few hundred pounds*
16	*(an Heiress)*
17[5]	*Has, from being a long time in trade acquired a little. Is in good credit but by [no] means rich*
18[6]	*Is merely a maker for Harvey Brand & Co. Has made a little money and very cautious. Property bonded*
28[7]	*A bold forward marcher. Speaks on all public occasions. Anti-Corn Law &c &c*
29	*Bankrupts owed £46,000. So involved in accommodation that £84,000 ranks on their estate 1/6 composition expected. Failed in 1826 paid 12/-*

PAISLEY. 17

1 Baird, William, grain merchant, Whitehaugh
2 Baird, Wm., spirit dealer, hay and straw retailer, 2 Wellmeadow
Baker, Archibald, carpet shoemaker, 8 Wellmeadow
4 Baking Association, baking house, 21 New Smithhills, John M'Gregor, foreman
Balderston, Andrew, grocer, 6 Barclay street
Baldrence, Andrew, 86 Canal street
7 Baldwin, Wm., smith and bell hanger, 6 St Mirren's street —house do.
8 Ballantyne, James, dyer, 5 Snodgrass Lane—house, 10 Barclay street
Ballantyne, Wm., cabinet maker, 19 Abbey close
Banks, Rev. James, house Mount Pleasant
Barbour, David, grocer and spirit dealer, 68 Canal street
12 Barbour, Robert, jun., umbrella and bandbox maker, furnishing shop, 9 St. Mirren street
13 Barbour, Robert, umbrella manufacturer, 101 High street
14 Barbour, William, wright and cabinet maker, 24 Causeyside—furniture warehouse and house do.
15 Barclay, James, silk and yarn merchant, 111 Causeyside —house, 3 Oakshaw head
Poor Barclay, James, spirit dealer, 6 West Croft street
Barclay, John, grocer, 10 Glen street
Dead Barclay, Mrs. Robert, of Glen, Canal Bank
Barr, Alexander, cowfeeder, 36 St. James street
Barr, Andrew, clerk, Adelphi mill, 68 New Sneddon
21 Barr, David & Co., dyers, 7 Marshall's lane
Barr, David, of Barr David & Co., house, 4 Clark's place
Barr, David, grocer and spirit dealer, 51 Caledonia street
24 Barr, George, leather merchant, 24 High street—house do.
Barr, James, grocer and spirit dealer, 12 New Sneddon
26 Barr, James, of Laigh Common—house 1 Maxwellton
Barr, James, wright and glazier, 77 High st.—ho. 79 do.
Barr, Janet, heddle caster, 15 Sir Michael street
Barr, John, assistant clerk, Adelphi mill, 68 New Sneddon
Barr, John, of Barr & M'Nab—house, 8 Abercorn street
Barr, John, clerk, Lounsdale
Barr, John, grocer, 8 Wallneuk street
Dead Barr, John K., grocer and tea dealer, 169 George street

B 2

Entry	**Page 17**
1	Poor. His father who died about 4 years ago was Bankrupt at the time
2	Oct 1841 Absconded. Nothing left behind
4	Has been in existence for 12 years. Has many partners. One Guinea shares and has returned in that time 26/- in dividends. A sore check on the Bakers in Paisley
7[1]	A good old established trade. A well doing hard working man in good credit but not rich
8[2]	Failed in 1835 as Wilson and Ballantyne and absconded. Came from America 2 years ago. In no credit, His old trick not forgiven
(10)	A very weak brother but [except] in opinion
12	Great drinker. Now joined the Teetottlers. Beware of him
13[3]	Father of the above. A quiet steady well behaved man, long in business. Not wealthy but highly respected
14[4]	Well doing man. Good trade. Must have made a little money, though hard up just now. Has a heavy stock of furniture on hand
15[5]	Has very considerable means, both got by his father and acquired himself, but having engaged in a heavy Iron concern at Skaterigg in company with his brother & Wm Galloway he will require all he has
(16)	Poor
(18)[6]	Dead
21	Failed in 1831 and again in 1841. Is a well doing man and industrious, but in a dangerous trade that has paid nobody these 20 years
24[7]	Failed 1841 Oct
26[8]	Has much House property in ordinary years about £800 of rental. Has had at this time to assist his son (4 next page) [Barr & McNab] liberally which with bad paid rents has made his cash scarce. Is wealthy. Has no bonds neither on houses nor vessels
(33)	Dead

18 PAISLEY.

Barr, John, jun., manufacturer, 13 Wardrop street—house 6 Stow street
Barr, John, muslin manufacturer, 72 Canal street
Barr, John, sen., feuar, 2 Dyer's wynd
Barr & M'Nab, iron founders, engineers, smiths, millwrights, and boiler makers, Abercorn Foundry, 15 North Croft street
Barr, Matthew, of Barr and Millar, house 51 Love street
Barr & Millar, cloth merchants, 9 High street
Barr & M'Neil, silk, woollen, and cotton dyers, 4 Bridge street, Newtown
Barr, Mrs. Alexander, Underwood street
Barr, Mrs. Janet, yarn merchant, 41 New street
Barr, Mrs. John, grocer and spirit dealer, 74 High street
Barr, Mrs., midwife, 69 Causeyside
Barr, Patrick, of Barr & Wilson—house 2 Garthland lane
Barr, Robert, chandler, 40 High street
Barr, Robert, grocer and cowfeeder, 26 Love street
Barr, Robert, Paisley Apothecary Hall, 8 High street and 25 Moss street
Barr, Thomas, Ramshorn tavern, 2 High street
Barr, William, jun., writer, 4 Moss st.—ho. 1 Maxwellton
Barr, William, writer, 33 Old Sneddon street—house Ferguslie place
Barr, William, cowfeeder, 17 Barclay street
Barr & Wilson, builders, 2 Garthland lane, & 7 Stow st.
Bartlemore, John, sheriff clerk's office, (County Buildings) —house 52 Love street
Bass, John, engineer and manager, Glasgow & Paisley joint railway, Gilmour st.— ho. station, (west side) do.
Bayne, William, excise officer, Johnston
Beat, John & Co., spirit dealers, 38 New street
Beat, Robert, of Beat and Sproul—ho. 90 George street
Beat & Sproul, smiths and farriers, 8 Christie street and 90 George street
Beaton, William, beamer, Lylesland
Begg, A., silk mercer and draper, 23 High st.—ho. 90 do.
Begg, James, grocer, 3 New street
Begg, John, teacher, 45 Maxwellton
Beith, Fulton, flesher, 30 Old Sneddon

Entry	**Page 18**
1[1]	*Has no means. A maker for Harvey Brand & Co. – and no credit*
2	*Out of business. Failed in 1835*
4[2]	*Has by much industry acquired a good large business which though for some years, it did not pay them has paid them well since the railway commenced. Have this year made a bad debt with Baird & Wallace £1800 which has crippled them. They have required the help of No.26 prior page Barr's father who says their whole is not gone by that debt but nearly so*
6	*Miller got some money from his father and Barr from his uncle and bought their predecessors stock in 1835. Are in good credit and <u>apparently</u> doing well*
7	*Never had any means. 3 years in trade 1841 Oct Bankrupt*
9	*30 years in the same shop. Had a black guard husband now dead. Has made nothing*
15[3]	*Has means left by his father. A good business, and some house property*
16[4]	*Has always a roaring house, but it does not pay him. Failed about 3 years ago*
17[5]	*Without means or business. Son of 26 prior page who supports him. A well informed sober young man but too soft to get on*
18[6]	*Has considerable means but from his style of living is supposed to be making poorer. A great politician – Town Councillor and Clerk of Supply for the County*
20	*Poor Poor Avoid them*
24	*Foreman mason at building Western Bank in 1837. Failed since in the grocery line*
26	*Long in trade but has done no good*
28[7]	*Is (1841 Dec) fairly beat out of business by the badness of trade. Is going to Glasgow with the little means he has left*
30[8]	*Shifts his place continually and fails occasionally, last time about 3 years ago*

Bell, Elizabeth, grocer, 1 Saucel
Bell, Henry, sheriff and town officer, 36 Moss street
Bell, John, carrier, (Glasgow,) 11 New Smithhills
Bell, Richard, manager, tan-work, 1 Seedhill—ho. 2 do.
Bell, Thomas, spirit dealer, 67 Canal street
Bell, William, surgeon, 19 George street
Bennie, William, musician, 21 Moss street
Berry, William, grocer and spirit dealer, 21 Orchard st.
Beveridge, Alexander, broker, 31 Cotton street
Bicket, William, feuar, 12 Barclay street
Biggar, Hugh, victualler, 82 Canal street
Biggar, John, bookseller, stationer, and librarian, 32 High street—house 82 do.
Biggar, Thomas, shawl manufacturer, 109 Causeyside
Bisset, Robert, shawl manufacturer, 11 Ferguslie
Bissland, John, cowfeeder, 1 Union street
Bissland, Miss, 34 Oakshaw street
Bissland, William, & Co., manufacturers, 5 Christie terrace
Bissland, Wm., of Bissland, Wm. & Co.—ho. 4 Orr square
Black, John, smith and farrier, Stonefield
Blackhall dyework receiving office, 24 Orchard street— John Gilchrist, dyer
Blackhall Factory office, 107 Causeyside, Harvey, Brand & Co.
Blackwood, Andrew, carter & cowfeeder, 8 Glen street
Blackwood, Misses, dress & corset makers, 6 Love street
Blaikie, Mrs Andrew, 7 Abbey street
Blair, Archibald, tailor, 89 High street
Blair & Gibson, manufacturers, 114 Causeyside
Blair, Henry, boot & shoemaker, 83 Canal street
Blair, Hugh, grocer, 56 Storie street
Blair, James, agent Glasgow railway, Gilmour st.—house 12 Saucel
Blair, James, spirit dealer & eating house, 25 New street
Blair, John, foreman at Keith Alex. & Co , 9 Shuttle st.
Blair, John, grocer, and spirit dealer, 32 Wellmeadow
Blair, John, spirit dealer and eating house, 6 Moss street
Blair, Mrs. Peter, grocer and spirit dealer, 6 George street
Blair, Peter, porter Glasgow Union Bank, 109 High street—house do.

Entry	**Page 19**
3	*Made a little money but lost it with his son in the Dy[e]ing business*
10[1]	*The introducers of the Shawl trade to Paisley 1808. Bickett & Linn & Thomson Bickett & Co. Has a little property bonded*
11	*A sergeant of Militia with a pension. No means*
12	*Left considerable means by his father but spent much of it in an indolent idle life. Is supposed to have been forced to begin business when his means were coming to a close*
13[2]	*Well-spoken of but could have no means to begin with and cannot have made much wealth*
14	*Provost of the Town last 3 years. Is reported to be easy in his business and has escaped well this year. Cannot be very wealthy*
17	*Wealthy old established trade conducted in a <u>caring</u> way with one foreman*
19	*Left considerable means by his Father last year*
21	*Glasgow firm of high repute in Paisley*
26	*1842 Bankrupt composition 4/6*

Blair, Robert, jun., tailor, 16 George street
Blair, Walter, grocer and spirit dealer, 1 Bridge street—spirit cellar, 1 Orchard street
Blair, William, joiner & cabinet maker, 30 Gauze street
Boag, Allan, shawl & plaid warehouse, 8 Broomlands
Bogle, Joseph Moore, clerk Glasgow Union Bank, 109 High street—house 57 Canal street
Bonar & Thomson, shawl manufacturers, 8 Orchard st.
Booz, John, patriarch to the House of Israel—house 30 Gauze street
Borland, Alexander, accountant, Western Bank of Scotland, 1 Forbes' place—house 59 Causeyside
Borland, Alexander, sen., feuar, 52 Canal street
Borland, A., tertius, clerk, Western Bank of Scotland, 1 Forbes' place—house 59 Causeyside
Borland, David, society officer, 33 Lady lane
Borland, John C., hair dresser, 69 Broomlands
Borland, Mrs., eating house, 5 Broomlands
Bowes, William, builder, 1 St. James' street
Bowie, James, bookseller, librarian and public reading room, 99 Causeyside
Bowie, Walter, farmer, Holland Bush
Bowie, William, keeper Victoria bowling green, 33 Lady lane
Boyd, James, window glazier, 32 High street—house 33 Oakshaw street
Boyd, John, egg and green store, 92 Causeyside
Boyd, John, upholsterer, 6 Smithhills
Boyd, Matthew, manuf., 6 Causeyside—ho. 8 Neilston st.
Boyd, Mrs., cowfeeder, 8 Neilston street
Boyd, Robert, manufacturer, 109 Causeyside—ho. 23 do.
Boyd, Thomas & Co., shawl warehouse, 116 Causeyside
Boyd, Thomas, of Boyd, Thomas & Co.—ho. 36 Causeyside
Boyd, Wm. & Son, merchants, 26 Gordon's lane—ho. do.
Boyd, Wm., jun., tea and sugar warehouse, 30 High st.—house 52 do.
Boyd, Wm., vintner, (carriers' quarters) 91 Causeyside
Boyle, James, wine and spirit dealer, (Sun Inn) 7 Moss st.
Bradley, James, shoemaker, 3 New Smithhills
Brand, Wm. of MacNair & Brand—ho. Barshaw

Entry	**Page 20**
2[1]	Bankrupt 1841 paid 12/-. Town councillor. Occasionally in an Asylum and never fully compusmentum
4	1841 Bankrupt No composition
6	Had a little money from their relations never got into the foolish speculations that the 2 last years produced. Cautious lads
14[2]	No means
15	Newly commenced. It will not do
18	Has been long in business. Means unknown but they cannot be great
20	[Blank]
21	Provost Boyd. Poor. Does very little business. Has some heritable property in Renfrew said to be bonded
23[3]	Supposed to be of the 1st class of manufacturers but is giving it up for the stuff trade. Must have considerable means in trade and a little house property. Has kept almost clear of the losses this year 1841
24	No means. A branch of his brother's trade (23 [Robert above]) Bankrupt composition 3/-
26[4]	In the Canada trade. Have some means but have nearly wrecked themselves 1841 with overspeculation
27	Easy in business. Brother of (23 [Robert above]). In good credit
29	Has some means and a good going business. Inland receipts from Western Bank[a]

---

[a] The phrase 'inland bill' is quite common in distinction to foreign bills of exchange. Allan Alexander Maconochie, regius professor of civil law at Glasgow in the 1840s, gave an entire lecture entitled 'inland bills' in session 1850/51, and foreign trade and inland trade are often compared. Inland bills imply inland receipts. NRS, SC6/83/1, lecture 58

PAISLEY. 21

Brannan, Hugh, shoemaker, 10 Canal street
Brannan, James, shoemaker and grocer, 86 New Sneddon
Bremner, Rev. John, Catholic Clergyman—house 2 East Buchanan street
Brewster, Rev. Patrick—house Hillhead
Brodie, John, broker, 18 Old Sneddon
Brodie, John, shoemaker, 72 Broomlands
Brodie, Robert, accountant, Paisley Commercial Bank—house 3 Glen street
Brodie, Thomas, spirit dealer, 14 St. Mirren street
Brodie, ---, warper, 6 Cumberland Court, 110 Causeyside
Brookes, James, wigmaker and haircutter, 18 Gauze st.
Brough, David, silk mercer, 109 High street—house 1 Garthland lane
Brough, Peter, of Brough & Sharp—ho. Oakshaw House, 42 Oakshaw street
Brough and Sharp, haberdashers, 96 High street
Brown, Allan, cabinet maker and weavers' wright, 10 Old Sneddon and 20 Causeyside
Brown, Andrew, carding master, Underwood mill
Brown, Andrew, clerk, Paisley Commercial Bank—house George place
Brown, Andrew, cotton spinner, Auchentorlie
Brown, Henry, broker and shoemaker, 76 High street
Brown, H. & J., manufacturers, 109 Causeyside
Brown, James, excise officer—house 140 George street
Brown, James, of Brown, Wm. jun. & Co.—ho. Blackhall
Brown, James, feuar, 3 East Croft street
Brown James S., governor, Town Hospital, 7 New Sneddon—house 2 Back Sneddon
Brown, James, jun., sheriff officer, 19 Moss street
Brown, James, sheriff officer, 8 Moss street
Brown, John, canteen, Paisley Barracks, Williamsburgh
Brown, John, M.D., 80 High street—ho. 1 Orr square
Brown, John, farmer, Alton
Brown, John, farmer, High Cardonald
Brown, John, flesher, 23 Gauze street—ho. 32 Cotton st.
Brown, John, grocer, 41 George street
Brown, John, grocer, 25 Queen street
Brown, John, manufacturer of hosiery, 26 High street

Entry	**Page 21**
3[1]	*Highly respected. A useful manager in all our public Institutions, Infirmary, Library &c &c*
4[2]	*A firey furious blockhead. A pest to the town. A learned man and an excellent preacher, which increases his power to do mischief*
11[3], 12[4]	*Sons of an old wealthy heritor in Kinross. Were made comfortable by their father and has improved it. Have considerable means, especially Peter in Gas, Water &c shares. And both eligible for Directors in the Paisley Commercial Bank*
13	*Sharp the principal shopman with Brough (Peter) now a small share for management Baillie Brough's time being much taken up with his other investments. A Tory Baillie & JP*
14	*Poor, failed this year in consequence of Holms & Andrews insolvency*
16	*Has very considerable means – the [son] of an old wealthy family – Brown & Brown & Sharps. A quiet well meaning lad without parts*
17[5]	*Left much wealth by his father. And made some years ago. Considerable himself and not withstanding his bad business surely has it yet*
18[6]	*Insolvent*
19[7]	*The partner got into the excise by means of Hastie M.P. nephew of Brown, Egypt Park – 22 next page*
26[8]	*An Ignorant Blustering Stupid Radical*
31	*Wealthy and a good business in the line*
32	*Succeeded to his father's old established business. Had means left him, but has now to contend with his sisters 4 next page*

Brown, John, salesman, Quarrelton Coal Basin, 29 Canal street—ho. 68 Love street
Brown, John, (tailors' house of call,) 32 Gauze street
Brown, John, wheelwright and turner, 62 High street
Brown, Miss, manufacturer of hosiery & shirts, 4 Moss st.
Brown, Misses, of Crossflat
Brown, Mrs. Andrew, George place
Brown, Mrs., furnishing shop, 39 High street
Brown, Mrs., grocer and spirit dealer, 18 Smithhills
Brown, Mrs. John, baker, 56 Causeyside
Brown, Mrs. John, farmer, Henderston
Brown, Neil, *theikar*, 71 High street
Brown and Polson, bleachers and woollen scourers, Thurscraig
Brown, Robert, grocer and spirit dealer, 37 Storie street
Brown, Robert, pattern drawer, 4 Castle street
Brown, Robert, Town Chamberlain, County Buildings— house 34 New Sneddon
Brown, Sharps, & Co., manufacturers, 166 George street
Brown, Thomas, beamer, 44 Storie street
Brown, William, baker, 6 Moss street
Brown, William, foreman at Lowndes, Wm. & J. & Co. —house 31 Glen street
Brown, William, gardener, 13 Gauze street
Brown, William, grocer, 9 Wardrop street
Brown, Wm., of Brown Wm. jun. & Co.—ho. Egypt Park
Brown, Wm. jun. & Co., shawl and yarn merchants, 108 Causeyside
Brown, William N., teacher, 12 Prussia street
Brown, William & Son, manufacturers, 10 Wardrop st.
Brown, Wm., of Urie & Brown—house 12 Neilston street
Brownlie, John & Co., spirit dealers, 1 Wellmeadow
Brownlie, William, hosier, 102 High street
Bruce, John, fishmonger, 12 Moss street and 106 Causeyside
Bryce, James, joiner and timber merchant, 13 Hunter st. —house 71 Love street
Bryce, John, iron merchant, 7 Dyers' wynd—house 34 Moss street
Buchan, Mrs., dress and corset maker, 29 New Sneddon
Buchanan, H., grocer, 51 George street

Entry	**Page 22**
4	*Daughter of an old established hosier. Had some money by her father. And has the best business in the line in the town.*
5	*(Wealthy)*
6[1]	*Ditto*
7	*Mother of 4 [and 5] above Has an annuity. In a small way*
8	*40 years in business. Has a good trade but is not known to have made money*
9[2]	*About 6 months a widow. A compound quietly taken at her husband's death*
12[3]	*Do a large business – too large for any means they can have. John Colquhoun's failure showed they dealt greatly in Bills – see Polson*
16	*An old established house, conducted on a modern commercial system. Very wealthy. Wm & Thos Sharp sons of old Sharp the only partners alive. See Sharps*
18	*Respectable but not wealthy. Brother [in law] of 9 [John Brown] above*
21[4]	*Conducted by the wife. See 25 [William Brown & Son] below*
22[5], 23[6]	*Insolvent. Paid this year 4/6 pr £. 4 years ago his balance showed £18,000 clear. A nephew with 1/8 share drove their trade to ruin. Much respected. The MP of the Town (Hastie) an old shopman of his when both were weaving in Paisley and has paid his composition in cash. Said to be a present for old friendship*
25	*Have failed often (though not this year) in 1825 and 1829 has much property so bonded that creditors cannot touch it. Poor see 21 [William Brown]*
30	*Has a tolerable share of the trade of the town but no means. Takes low estimates. Railway has gone through his workshop & yard which has been no doubt a windfall in time of need*

Buchanan, Hugh, grocer, 25 Well street
Buchanan, James, gas inspector, 10 New street
Buchanan, James, spirit dealer, 3 Lillias' wynd
Buchanan, James, wine and spirit merchant, 162 George street, house 19 Storie street
Buchanan, John, warper, 10 New street
Buchanan, Misses, milliners and dressmakers, 56 Causeyside
Buchanan, Moses, boot and shoemaker, 2 Maxwell st.
Buchanan, Mrs. James, house 55 High street
Buchanan, Walter, late merchant, Carriagehill House
Buchanan, Walter, of Buchanan, Walter, & Co.—house Haircraig's cottage
Buchanan, Walter, & Co., woollen, silk, & calico printers, Blackland mill
Buchanan, William, baker, 70 Causeyside
Bulley, John, cashier Western Bank of Scotland, 1 Forbes' place—house do.
Bulloch, John, hair dresser & umbrella maker, 43 Moss st.
Burgess, Charles, manufacturer, 169 George street—house 57 Canal street
Burgess, Jas., porter to the British Linen Company's Bank —house 37 Thread street
Burgess, Robert, grocer and spirit dealer, 136 George st.
Burgess, Thomas, contractor and well digger, 9 Ferguslie
Burns, Miss Janet, flesher, Gilmour street
Burns, Rev. Robert, D.D.—house Camphill
Burns, William, 17 West street
Burnside, Mrs., broker, 11 Old Sneddon st.

CAIRNS, Rev. Robert, U. S. C.—house Camphill
Calderwood, James, boot and shoemaker, 85 High street
Caldwell, David, & Co., seedsmen and fruit dealers, 73 Broomlands
Caldwell, George, sen., bookseller, stationer, and printer, 2 New street (up one stair)—house Teetotal Tower, West Sandyford
Caldwell, James, pattern drawer at M'Kechnie, Kerr, & Co.—house 95 Causeyside
Caldwell, James, writer, 6 Moss st.—ho. Fairhill, Calside
Caldwell, John, Abbey house factor, 11 Abbey close

Entry	**Page 23**
3	Poor. Disreputable house. Soldiers rendezvous
4	Old Baillie Buchanan. Highly respectable but not wealthy. Failed in 1822 as a manufacturer. Has acquired an excellent family trade. Has some property which rents well. Apparently prospering
9[1]	Beat out of business. Now living on £40 or £50 reversion of rents over bond interest and the gifts of his sons who are said to be doing well in India
10	Insolvent this year. A very ignorant person and has not ability to succeed in anything
11	[Blank, with 10]
12	Newly opened. No means. Will not succeed
14	Poor as a Church mouse
15	Has some means though not great. With the exception of £160 with Turnbull of London has escaped the crisis of these years. Steady careful. No family and may succeed
17	Failed in 1832. Very poor and ever will be
19[2]	Poor Poor the remains of an old highly respected family
20[3]	Forward, bustling, meddling body. A leader of the Non-Intrusion party. Wealthy
23[4]	No cash, but said to be a first rate preacher
26[5]	Wealthy, a good business. Has allowed his wife to dissipate a few thousand pounds on a gee gaw of no earthly use on Renfrew Road[a]
28[6]	Had once a good business, but through inat[t]ention (& drink) has lost it.[b] Has some property bonded. Poor though always blustering about his wealth
29	Poor. Insolvent manufacturer

---

[a] Teetotal Tower. For an amusing description of this building and Mrs Caldwell, see John Urie, *Reminiscences of Eighty Years,* Paisley, Gardner, 1908, p.33, quoted in Appendix II.

[b] This seems to be a rare occasion when Borland is referring to the wrong person: he is probably describing the father of James Caldwell the writer, who was a grocer in Paisley.

Caldwell, John, manufacturer, 7 St. Mirren street—house 12 Neilston street
Caldwell, John & Son, tailors, 48 Storie street
Caldwell, Mrs. Robert, feuar, Carriagehill
Caldwell, Robert, grocer, 12 Neilston street
Caldwell, William, shoemaker and agent for Ross's blacking, 30 St. James' street
Callender, Alex. & Co., rag and waste merchants, 2 New street—house 43 do.
Callender, James, grocer, 120 George street
Callender, Peter, teacher, 3 Marshall's lane
Callender, Thomas, currier and leather merchant, 23 and 25 Thread street—house 13 do.
Cameron, Christina, grocer, 11 Cotton street
Cameron, Daniel, porter, 101 Causeyside
Cameron, Daniel, surveyor of works and collector of statute labour money for Newtown—house 10 Prussia st.
Cameron, David, ropemaker, 84 High street
Cameron, Duncan, spirit dealer, 10 Moss street—ho. do.
Cameron, Gaven, carding master, Underwood mill
Cameron, Hugh, broker, 74 High street
Cameron, Hugh, jun., wine and spirit dealer, 2 Cotton st.
Cameron, Hugh, wholesale wine and spirit merchant, 6 Cotton street
Cameron, James, flesher, 8 Love street
Cameron, John, grocer and victualler, 24 New street
Cameron, John, rag and waste store, 22 New street
Cameron, John, ropemaker, 73 High street
Cameron, John, spirit dealer, 21 Moss street
Cameron, John, spirit dealer, 86 New Sneddon
Cameron, Mrs., baker, 25 High street
Cameron, Mrs. Daniel, weavers' office, 76 High street
Cameron, Miss Sarah, furnishing and hosiery, 8 New st.
Cameron, Peter, goods' agent for Glasgow Railway, Gilmour street—house King street, Saucel
Cameron, Robert, teacher, 12 West street
Campbell, Alexander, of Barnhill, Sheriff-substitute—ho. 6 Garthland place
Campbell, Alex., boot and shoemaker, 12 St James' place
Campbell, Arch., mercht. tailor and grocer, 30 Causeyside

Entry	**Page 24**
1	*A scion of a very wealthy family by the mother's side Wm McAlister and sons. Has money among his houses and is assisted by his uncle, but who does not avow himself to be a partner. A well doing trade*
2[1]	*Poor Poor Father & Mother of 28 [James Caldwell] prior page*
3	*Plenty of means, strangely acquired by her father*
4	*Father of No.1 [John Caldwell]. His wife wealthy in her own right*
5	*Poor Poor an old decayed tradesman*
6	*Insolvent 1840 as a grocer and no better yet*
7	*Ditto ditto*
9[2]	*Respectable, Good business, easy in circumstances*
13[3]	*Poor see 22 [Archibald Cameron] a brother*
14	*Considerable means both in business and lent out – some property*
17	*Disreputable character never solvent*
18[4]	*Was in 1830 worth £4,000. Lost much of it in foolish cautionary and law expenses and the rest of it in foolish credits 1841 December insolvent. Settlement of 10/- per £ owes £830. Cost of his pro £1,900 Bond £1,000*
19	*Poor – much insolvent*
20[5]	*Excellent run easy in business*
22	*Poor see 13 [David Cameron] a brother*
30[6]	*Has been SS since 1802. A good but lazy judge. Highly respected and keeps aloof from the public. Considerable means left him, reputed wealth £15,000*
32[7]	*No great means but easy Industrious wife in grocery. Lost £200 by his son this year who would be a manufacturer [of] linen and failed*

Campbell, D. & D., silk, cotton, and woollen dyers, 59 New Sneddon—house do.
Campbell, Daniel, tailor, 43 New street
Campbell, Duncan, spirit dealer, 16 Moss street
Campbell & Gillespie, agents and messengers at arms, 25 Old Sneddon
Campbell & Gilmour, plumbers and gas fitters, 42 High st.
Campbell, James, foreman to James Stirrat, 61 High st.
Campbell, James, spirit dealer, 22 Causeyside
Campbell, James, grocer, 14 Cotton street
Campbell, Janet, cowfeeder, 3 North Croft street
Campbell, John, broker, 19 Old Sneddon
Campbell, John, of Campbell & Gilmour— ho. 65 Canal st.
Campbell, John, feuar, 3 North Croft street
Campbell, John, fishmonger, 100 Causeyside—house 30 Storie street
Campbell, John, of Stirling, Wm. & Co.—ho. 99 High st.
Campbell, John, wine and spirit merchant, 76 Broomlands —house 19 Queen street
Campbell, Miss, teacher, 13 Wardrop street
Campbell, Mrs. Alexander, cowfeeder, 4 New Sneddon
Campbell, Mrs. Daniel, cowfeeder, 61 Back Sneddon
Campbell, Mrs. Edward, Greenlaw Cottage
Campbell, Mrs. John, furnished lodgings, 3 Garthland st.
Campbell, Mrs. R. (Temperance Coffee House) 9 High st.
Campbell, Paul, bleacher and general washing field, Lonend
Campbell, Rev. John, 44 Oakshaw street
Campbell, Robert, broker, 80 Broomlands
Campbell, Robert, wine and spirit merchant, 23 Lawn st.
Campbell, Thomas, of Campbell & Gillespie—ho. 2 Caledonia street
Campbell, Wm., shawl manufacturer, 3 Cumberland Court, 110 Causeyside—house 30 do.
Campbell, William, teacher, 2 Gauze street
Campsie, Thomas, North Church officer, 69 Love street
Carlile, Alex., of Carlile, James & Sons—house 76 New Sneddon
Carlile, George, feuar, Niddry street
Carlile, James, & Sons, thread manufs. 13 Carlile place

Entry	**Page 25**
1[1]	*Careful industrious good tradesman. Made in the last 7 years considerable means, the greater part of which must now by the failures of this year, be swept away*
4	*The only messengers in the town. Have an excellent business. Have not acquired much means as yet, say 4 or 5 hundred pounds which is lent on bond*
5[2]	*Newly commenced. Concern will not go Means unknown Any they have will be lost*
15	*Better known by Burdy Campbell an ignorant blustering uneducated person. A town councillor. Has acquired means £1,200 or £1,500 it is said*
22	*Ignorant political leader of Chartism without a penny to bless himself with*
23	*Quiet inoffensive man never heard of in the general public. Gaelic preacher*
27	*Son of Archibald Campbell prior page. Insolvent*
30[3], 32[4]	*Sole partner of 32 [James Carlile]. The remains of a highly respected old trader in the same premises since 1740. Has means but must have dispensed a considerable part of them in Househill Iron speculation on which he was (and is) a foolish enthusiast*

Carlile, Thomas, of Carlile, Wm. & Co.—ho. 33 New Sneddon
Carlile, William, of Carlile, William & Co.—ho. 33 New Sneddon
Carlile, William, & Co. manufacturers, 22 Moss street
Carmichael, Charles, farmer, Hunterhill
Carmichael, John, flesher and grocer, 30 Cotton street
Carrick, James, grocer and cooper, 45 Millerston
Carruth, Alexander, cooper, 58 Causeyside
Carruth, George, hosier, 5 Abbey close
Carswell, Allan, of Glen, Anderson, & Co.—house Short Roods, Nethercommon
Carswell, David, bookbinder, 14 St. Mirren street—house 13 St. James' place
Carswell & Gardner, manufacturers, 1 New Sneddon
Carswell, James, ginger beer manufacturer, 79 High st.
Carswell, Miss, 83 High street
Carswell, Robert, Short Roods, Nethercommon
Carswell, Thomas, of Carswell & Gardner—house Springbank cottage, Love street
Cathcart, John, general grocer, tea, wine and spirit merchant, 16 High street—house 77 do.
Cathcart, Mrs. Alex., grocer & spirit dealer, 6 Wallace st.
Chalmers, J. K., teacher, 7 West brae
Chalmers, James, spirit dealer, 4 Old Sneddon
Chalmers, Tarbet, grocer and vintner, 13 Maxwellton
Chalmers, William, shoemaker, 10 New Sneddon
Chillas, Mrs. Robert, 4 Garthland street
Chillas, Robert, 2 Caledonia street *Spirit merchant*
Christie, John, saddler, 50 Moss street
Christie, William, grocer, 49 Causeyside
Christie, William, teacher, 1 Neilston road
Clapperton, John, & Co., thread manufs., 70 New Sneddon
Clapperton, John, of Clapperton, John, & Co.—ho. 60 Love street
Clara, Philip, broker, 10 Lawn street
Clark, Andrew, warper, 4 Abbey close—ho. 25 Niddry st.
Clark, Daniel, boot and shoemaker, 9 Lawn street
Clark, Jas., of Clark, J. & J. & Co.—ho. Chapel House
Clark, John, grocer, 44 Moss street

Entry	**Page 26**
1[1], 2, 3[2]	*1, 2, 3 [Thomas, William] Cousins of 32 prior page [James Carlile]. Wealthy. An excellent business, long established, and highly respectable. In the light or fancy silk line. No opposition in Paisley*
7	*Poor. Only one year in trade*
10	*Insolvent 1841*
11[3]	*Has a good business Carswell wealthy and Gardner industrious and active*
12[4]	*Poor Poor Insolvent 1838*
14	*Wealthy retired*
15	*Much means both in house property, shares and in trade. A cautious man*
16	*In good credit. Not wealthy but easy in means and industrious*
19	*Always hard up, and bills paid slow. Is said he got property at his mother's death but it must be inconsiderable*
23[5]	*Spirit merchant. Insolvent 1841. Composition 10/-*
24[6]	*Respectable. Good business. easy*
27[7]	*Commenced in May 1834. Paterson a blustering partner, since put out. Son of Rev. J Clapperton Johnston[e][8]. Not wealthy but is said to have succeeded well*
30	*Brother of 32 [James] Poor Poor*
32[9]	*Very wealthy see No.2 [J & J Clark] next page*
33	*Failed 1829 and has not recovered. Poor. A precocious blockhead*

PAISLEY. 27

Clark, John, of Clark, J. & J. & Co.—ho. Burns' place
2   Clark, J. & J. & Co., thread manufacturers, counting house
        and factory, 3 Clark's place, Seedhill
    Clark, Miss, dressmaker and milliner, 44 Moss street
    Clark, Miss Ann, dressmaker, 148 George street
5   Clark, Wm., warper, 4 Abbey close—ho. 10 Cotton st.
    Cleland, Jas., gas inspector, 22 Moss street—ho. 70 Love st.
    Cleland, William, surgeon, accoucheur, and apothecary,
        from Glasgow apothecaries' hall—Sneddon dispensary,
        7 Old Sneddon
8   Climie, Robert, civil engineer and surveyor, 101 High st.
9   Clyde and Cochrane, shawl manufacturers, 116 Causeyside
    Clyde, Wm., of Clyde and Cochrane—ho. 12 Neilston st.
    Coats, George, of Coats and Shaw—house Saucel bank
    Coats, Jas., jun., of Coats, J. & P.—house 16 Maxwellton
13 Coats, James, sen., late manufacturer—house 11 Back
        row, Ferguslie
14 Coats, J. & P., thread manufacturers, Ferguslie
    Coats, Peter, of Coats, J. & P.—house 10 West brae
16 Coats & Shaw, manufacturers, 7 St. Mirren street
    Coats, Thos., of Coats J. & P.—house, 16 Maxwellton
18 Coats, William, grocer and ham curer, 68 Broomlands—
        house 5 William street
19 Cochran, Adam, gardener, Calside
    Cochran, Alex., manager at Brown & Polson's, Thurscraig
    Cochran, Andrew, spirit dealer, Carriagehill
22 Cochran, James, builder, grocer, and spirit dealer, 14
        Thread street
    Cochran, James, surgeon and oculist, 17 Wellmeadow
    Cochrane, James, teacher of dancing, 13 George street—
        Academy, 4 Smithhills—open from Nov. till March
    Cochran, John, feuar, Patterhill
    Cochran, John, glazier, 6 Old Sneddon
    Cochran, John, mashman, Saucel distillery, King street,
        Saucel
    Cochrane, Mat., of Clyde and Cochrane—house 9 Well-
        meadow
29 Cochran, Mrs., druggist, 26 Wellmeadow
    Cochran, Mrs., midwife, 14 Williamsburgh
31 Cochran, Mrs. William, eating house, 47 High street

Entry	**Page 27**
2[1]	*Excellent business inherited and improved. Much excellent house property and otherwise wealthy. James Stewart the brother in law retired but has not advertised out*
5	*Brother of No.2 [J & J Clark]. A small thatched house from his father. Poor*
8[2]	*Husband of Mrs Paton who having a good business in her first husband's name still retains it. Climie a good business*
9	*Insolvent. Composition 9/- 1840*
13[3]	*Out of business directly 20 years, and indirectly as the partner of James Bligh jun. & Co 7 years, from which as sleeping partner he took £8,000. The writer of this was consulted at the separation*
14	*J & P, the sons of 13 [James Coats senior], had a loan from their father (1831) from whom they rent their works. Are said to have done well*
16	*1842 Insolvent. Composition 12/6*
18[4]	*Old established trade. No great means realized but easy*
19[5]	*Gardener, herbalist and quack doctor. Poor*
22	*Disreputable character. Always to be avoided*
29[6]	*Considerable property made by her husband. Authoress of 'Memoirs of Milford'[a]*
31	*Poor. Her husband a butcher nicknamed Pudding Will stabbed one of his children to death by accident, which brooded on his mind & killed him 1841*

---

[a] No reference has been found for this book.

Cochran, Robert, feuar, 25 Old Sneddon
Cochran, Robert, merchant, 6 Cumberland Court, 110 Causeyside—house 2 St. James' street
Cochrane, William, clerk Saucel distillery, King street— house 2 Saucel
Cochran, Wm., carter and cowfeeder, 22 New Smithhills
Cochran, William, clock maker, 19 Smithhills
Cochran, Wm., eating house, ales, &c., 20 Wellmeadow
Cochran, William, enterer, 39 George street
Cochran, William, joiner, cabinet maker, and window glazier, 35 High street
Cockburn, John, spirit dealer, 110 George street
Coffee and News Room, 107 High street, (Cross,) James Love, keeper
Colquhoun, James, excise officer, Neilston street
Colquhoun, James, keeper West toll bar
Colquhoun, John, calenderer and bleacher, 10 Bridge street (burgh)—house do.
Colquhoun, John, clothlapper, 13 New st.—ho. 12 do.
Colquhoun, John, wine and spirit dealer, 9 North Croft st.
Colquhoun, Mrs. Jn., vegetable and fruit shop, 16 Geo. st.
Colquhoun, Mrs. Walter, stay maker, Gilmour street
Colquhoun, Walter, accountant and house factor, 5 Christie terrace—house 2 Garthland lane
Colquhoun, William, foreman, gas works—house do.
Colquhoun, William, sub-collector for Paisley water Co , —house 17 Wellmeadow
Comrie, Duncan, copper and tinsmith, 90 High street
Comrie, Peter, boot and shoemaker, 71 Broomlands
Comrie, Peter, cowfeeder, 4 West Campbell street
Condie, John C., bookbinder and paper ruler, 6 Christie terrace—house 38 New street
Connell, Adam, beamer, 43 Broomlands
Connell, Andrew, mason, furnace boiler builder, and smoke doctor, 14 Gauze street
Connell, Daniel, sheriff and town officer, and town crier, 2 Hunter street
Connell, John, baker, 36 High street
Connolly, Thomas, grocer and spirit dealer, 5 Inkle st.
Connor, Francis, travelling merchant, 98 High street

Entry	**Page 28**
1[1]	*Named Thornly to distinguish him from No.2 [Robert] from a free farm left him by a younger unmarried brother. Is in no business. Has means but being a sporting character is supposed to be making poorer*
2[2]	*Once the jun. partner of the far famed South American house, Robert Cochran & Sons owners of several ships. Failed in 1826. Has some means left. A respectable man, not in business, living on rents and Wife's annuity – Adam Keir, Bankers, daughter*
13[3]	*Over speculated in property. Made immense bad debts in business 1840 & 1841 Failed April 41 composition 9/- Dec 1841 sequestrated*
15	*Does not attend to his business. Horse trotter. House frequented by the sporting boys of the whole town. Always hard up. Might do well, has an excellent place*
18	*An old teacher. Very poor*
24	*In every public situation when gratuitous services are requested. Commissioner of Cart, Inspector of Hospital &c &c No means but a fair going trade*
28	*Has an excellent trade. Easy in means, not wealthy, but in considerable credit. A superior tradesman*

Cook, Archibald, engineer and manager of gas work—house do.
Cook, Christina, grocer, 12 George street
Cook, James, brush, basket, and toy warehouse, 39 High street, and 3 Moss street
Cook, James, manufacturer, 6 Forbes place—ho. Garthland street
Cook, James, victualler, 9 Orchard street—house do.
Cook, John, pattern drawer, 26 Broomlands
Cormie, James, spirit cellar, 2 St Mirren street
Couper, James, carter and cowfeeder, 1 Barclay street
Couper, Robert, broker, 23 Abbey street
Couper, Thomas, shoemaker, 3 Oakshaw street
Cowan, Alexander, shoemaker, 10 Wellmeadow
Cowan, Henry, pawnbroker, 26 Wellmeadow
Cowan, James, baker, 81 Canal street
Cowan, Mrs. William, flesher, 20 Sandholes
Craies, Wm., clerk, Bank of Scotland—ho. 117 Causeyside
Craig, Alex., of Gibson and Craig—ho. 33 Oakshaw st.
Craig, Alex., Tradeston mills, Glasgow—meal and flour warehouses, 26 High st., and 19 Houstoun square, Johnstone
Craig, Arch., of Donald and Craig—ho. 8 Abercorn st.
Craig, David, writer, 5 Christie terrace—ho. Burns' place
Craig's drug shop, 102 Causeyside
Craig, James, merchant, Nethercommon
Craig, James and Co., brick, drain, and roofing tile makers, Greenock road, and Nethercommon
Craig, James, grocer, 50 Caledonia street
Craig, John, carter, 131 George street
Craig, John, spirit dealer, 79 Causeyside
Craig, John, surgeon, 82 High street—house 85 do.
Craig, Miss, 42 High street
Craig, Miss, milliner and straw hat maker, 18 Storie st.
Craig, Mrs., beamer, 7 West Croft street
Craig, Mrs., fish retailer, 13 Moss street
Craig, Mrs., grocer, 3 Love street
Craig, Mrs., midwife, 30 Gauze street
Craig, Mrs. Wm., grocer and spirit dealer, 56 High street
Craig, Rob., joiner and cartwright, 5 Back row, Sandholes

c 2

Entry	**Page 29**
1	*Famed as an engineer and discoverer of many refinements in making gas, but never sober*
4[1]	*Failed in 1826 paid 6/8 again in 1841 offers 2/-*
5[2]	*A triffling trade, purchased the property he is in with means from his father. Has feued a part of it to Holms & Andrew for a public work at a feu duty which pays the whole. That company having been sequestrated the building will soon fall into his hands by being swallowed up with feu duty*
12	*Has means in fee if his mother the life renter was dead Disreputable character. He will soon finish them. Trading on his mother's [14 below, Mrs William] money*
13	*Poor Poor no credit*
14[3]	*Mother of 12 [Henry] Life renter, dangerous*
19	*A mystery how he supports himself*
21, 22	*Sole partner of James Craig, brickmaker [22] stopped in 1835 owing to the confusion of his trade caused by a drunken son. On examination found he could pay all, and did so. Dangerous, beware*
25	*Not trustworthy*
26[4]	*Is said to be the richest surgeon in Paisley. Occasionally goes deranged*

Craig, William, spirit merchant, 26 Causeyside
Crawford, Alexander, agent for Mordant and Black iron liquors, 1 Renfrew street
Crawford, Andrew & Co., manufacturers, 116 Causeyside
Crawford, Duncan, spirit dealer, 62 Storie street
Crawford, Hugh, joiner and weavers' wright, 4 Queen st.
Crawford, James, cowfeeder, 13 Storie street
Crawford, James, professor of dancing—Academy, Lyceum Rooms, 101 High street (open from October till March)—house 33 High street
Crawford, Jas., wood turner, 23 Smithhills, entry by 20 do.
Crawford, John, accountant, agent for the Phœnix Fire Insurance Co., and Scottish Amicable Life Insurance Co., 5 Christie terrace—house 4 Stow place
Crawford, John, wright, 28 Causeyside
Crawford, Matthew, whinstone quarrier, 19 Mill street
Crawford, Miss, teacher of music, 24 Abbey street
Crawford, Mrs. D., glass, china, and earthenware merchant, 48 Moss street
Crawford, Mrs. John, spirit dealer, 5 St. Mirren street
Crawford, Mrs., straw hat and dressmaker, 109 George st.
Crawford, Ninian, of Crawford, Andrew, & Co.—house Glen lane cottage
Crawford, Wm., of Crawford, Andrew, & Co.—house 3 Back Sneddon
Crichton, Thos., jun., commercial traveller, Burns' place
Crichton, Thomas, sen., clerk, town hospital, 7 New Sneddon—house 10 Back Sneddon—session clerk for High Church parish
Crooks, John, carter, 131 George street
Crooks, John, carter, 23 Lady lane
Crooks, John, precentor U.S.C. Church (No. 2)—house 5 Inkle street
Cross, Andrew, trunk, travelling equipment, and umbrella manufacturer, 18 High street
Cross, James, shawl manufacturer, 116 Causeyside
Cross, Mrs., muslin printer, 18 High street
Cross, William, carver and gilder, 3 Gauze street
Crossley, James, silk, cotton, and woollen dyer, Cumberland place, Laigh Kirk lane

Entry	**Page 30**
2[1]	*Introducer of the imitation shawl trade to Paisley 1807. An old man drawing out a wretched existence*
3[2]	*Wealthy, Andrew retired and living on his means. Ninian (16 below) the only partner drawing profits. Respectable Individually*
7[3]	*Has had great income but has spent it all. Deep drinker and extravagant*
8	*Son of Alexander Crawford Poor. Endeavouring to obtain a living*
9[4]	*In 1818 partner of large concern Caldwell & Crawford failed that year. Failed 1826 Always in poverty by extravagant wife who is occassionally in Fancy farm[a]*
10	*Poor Poor*
13	*Sister in law of 3 and 16 [Andrew and Ninian] given a shop rent free out of compassion. Poor*
14[5]	*Well known ale house (Captain Crawford's) good <u>rum</u> – considerable property. Crawford's Club in Paisley equal to Brookes in London. Admission by ballot*
16[6]	*Sole partner though Andrew never advertised out. Have much valuable property held jointly. Highly respectable*
17	*Not a Partner merely manager or clerk*
24[7]	*Failed in 1840 Has done no good since*
27	*Merely Dyer to McKerrell & Morgan*

---

[a] Fancy Farm, near Gourock, was declared empty in the 1841 census and again in the 1845 New Statistical Account of Scotland for Inverkip, where it is recorded as belonging to General Duncan Darroch. It may well have been used as a controlled environment for the mentally ill.

Crossley, Michael & Co., dye-wood chipping and grinding mills, and preparers of printers' liquors, 11 Well street
Crossley & M'Master, dyers, 2 Saucel
Cumming, Moses, carter, 19 Lady lane
Cumming, Peter, spirit dealer, 16 Maxwellton street
Cumming, Thomas, cowfeeder, 32 Castle street
Cunningham, Daniel, ironmonger, 21 High st.—house do.
Cunningham, James, grocer, 26 Glen street
Cunningham, John, baker, 25 Gordon's lane
Cunningham, John, ironmonger, 88 High street—ho. do.
Cunningham, John, manufacturer, 31 Orchard street
Cunningham, John, spirit dealer, 60 Causeyside
Cunningham, Misses, milliners, 13 High street
Cunningham, Mrs. and Misses, boarding and day school, 26 High street
Cunningham, Mrs., milliner and straw hat maker, 3 Causeyside
Cunningham, Robert, 47 High street
Curr, William, flesher, 18 Smithhills
Currie, Alexander, clerk, at Glen, Anderson & Co.'s, 34 Gordon's lane
Currie, David, church officer, 39 Oakshaw street
Currie, David, shoemaker, 6 Williamsburgh
Currie, Findlay, cowfeeder, 11 School wynd
Currie, Jean, mangler, 2 Canal street
Currie, Mrs. Adam, spirit dealer, 12 Back Sneddon
Currie, Mrs. William, grocer and spirit dealer, 14 Seedhill
Currie, William, grocer and spirit dealer, 4 Renfrew st.
Cuthbertson, James, picking master, Underwood mill
Cuthbertson, Miss Jean, dressmaker, 7 Love street
Cuthbertson, Robert, hosiery and furnishings, 81 Broomlands
Cuthbertson, Thomas, silk merchant, 14 Causeyside
Cuthill, A., clerk at Coats, J. and P.—house 13 Ferguslie

DAISLEY, William, shoemaker, 1 Abbey close
Dalziel, David, flower lasher, 6 Cumberland Court, 110 Causeyside

Entry	**Page 31**
1	*Small means but are doing well. The partner McGibbon, having by means of his uncle the command of money when it is needed*
2	*No means. Not in credit. Always hard up*
5[1]	*Rather better than the ordinary class of cowfeeder*
6[2]	*Respectable has in ordinary times a good business. Has some valuable property*
9	*Brother of 6 [Daniel] and the same character*
10[3]-11	*One person. Insolvent. In jail for Cessio*[7]
16	*No means. Nor business, respectable*
22[4]	*Poor Poor*
28	*Of his own account worth nothing merely an agent for Harvey Brand & Co*

---

[7] For cessio bonorum, see Introduction p. xvi

PAISLEY.

Dalziel, John, wholesale stationery twine & thread warehouse, 6 Cumberland Court, 110 Causeyside
Dalziel, Mrs. Andrew, victualler and spirit dealer, 13 Canal street
Dalziel, Mrs., dressmaker, 122 George street
Davidson, Arthur, manufacturer, 29 Thread street
Davidson, John, beamer, 55 George street
Davidson, John, teacher of English and writing, 3 St. James' street
Davidson, Matthew, cowfeeder, 5 Newton street
Davidson, Miss—house 3 Orr square
Davidson, Thomas C., silk mercer & draper 16 High st.
Davidson, Thomas, salesman, at Baird & Wallace—house 89 Causeyside
Davis, James, farmer, North Cardonald
Davlin, James, broker, 70 High st.
Deans, Andrew, house 20 Orchard street
Dempster, Mrs., dressmaker, 4 Glen street
Denny, Joseph, wright and glazier, 7 Smithhills
Dick, John, at Dick, Walter & Son—house Greenhill House
Dick, Miss C., dressmaker, 31 Storie street
Dick, Thomas, of Dick, Walter, & Son—ho. Greenhill ho.
Dick, Walter, and Son, shawl warehouse, 9 Causeyside
Dickie, James, late grocer, Barterholm
Dickie, John, clothlapper, 4 Forbes' place—ho. 28 New st.
Dickson, David, grocer, 3 Renfrew street
Directory Office, 57 Canal street, Fowler, George, publisher, bookseller & bookbinder
Dixon, Miss—house, 13 Lawn street
Dobie, William, tobacconist and tallow chandler, 12 High street—house 34 Oakshaw street
Dobson, J., foreman, at Watson P. & T., 11 High street
Docherty, Charles, chimney sweep, 19 Old Sneddon
Donald and Craig, engineers, millwrights, and machine makers, 8 Renfrew street
Donald, J.K., bookkeeper, railway Gilmour street—house 36 High street
Donald, William, of Donald & Craig—house 8 West Croft street

Entry	**Page 32**
1[1]	*Small paltry concern. Without knowledge of the people he intends to supply, being newly commenced. Will lose the 30 or 40 pounds he has saved by firm industry*
4[2]	*Has been 17 years John Mair & Co agent. Small means, but not the knowledge of modern business. Respectable man*
9	*One of a lot of boys who within the last few years have set up dashy shops in the High street to the great hurt of the decent established traders. The present times will finish the whole of them*
13[3]	*An old broken down manufacturer – <u>Baillie Deans</u>. Living by house factorage but does not like to acknowledge the employment*
19	*Insolvent. Debts, real, £84,000. Accommodation and real £136,000 Composition 10/6 Made up in the most discreditable way by large purchases on the eve of failing*
21[4]	*A well behaved man doing his utmost but must be at or below par by the losses he has sustained*
25[5]	*Has considerable means. Long established and good trade. Once McLean & Dobie who as a company were wealthy. McLean died out*
28	*Large business, but the wonder is that they have not declared insolvency. The losses they have sustained this year have been immense*

Donald, William, foreman, at Lowndes, William & James & Co.—house 9 Wallace street
Donaldson, George, eating house, 15 Gauze street
d —Donaldson, Jas., boot and shoemaker, 18 Wellmeadow
Donaldson, James, cowfeeder, 28 Love street
Donaldson, Jas , shuttle maker, and locksmith, 18 Moss st.
Donaldson, John, smith, iron plough maker, and licensed veterinary surgeon, 64 Love street
Donaldson, Samuel, wright and mortcloth keeper for Abbey parish, 3 Thread street
Donaldson, William, boot and shoemaker, 27 St. James' street
Dougal, John, manager, Underwood cotton works
Dougal, John, umbrella maker, 5 George street
Douglas, John, boot and shoemaker, Carriagehill
Douglas, Margaret, eating house, 20 Sandholes
13 — Downie, John, shawl manufacturer, 169 George street
Downie, Martin, excise officer—house Glenpatrick
14—Downie, Mrs. Charles, Rosebank cottage, Calside
Downie, W., lappet wheel cutter and turner, 10 Oakshaw st.
Drennan, Robert, boot and shoe maker, 4 Broomlands
18 — Drummond, James, architect, 5 Christie Terrace—house 33 Old Sneddon
19 —Drummond, James, tea dealer, 12 Barclay street
70 — Drummond, Robert, & Co., grocers and spirit dealers, 72 Canal street
71 —Drummond, William, merchant, 2 Wardrop street—house 8 George street
72 —Duff, Daniel, watch and clock maker, and repairer of repeating watches, musical clocks and boxes, 16 High st.
73 —Duff, Robert, jun., general wholesale waste dealer, 2 Bridge street (New Town)—house 10 Abbey street
24 —Duff, Robert, rag and rope store, 3 Bridge street, (New Town)—house do.
Duffas, Thomas, excise officer—house 18 Gauze street
Dunbar, Archd., tinplate worker, and gasfitter, 86 High st.
Dunbar, David, boot and shoemaker, 4 Gauze street
76 —Duncan, David, gardener, Hope Temple gardens, 15 Love street
Duncan, John, letter runner—house 14 Back Sneddon

Entry	**Page 33**
3[1]	*Industrious, but no means*
13[2]	*Insolvent. Had means, but was finished by Dick*
15[3]	*General Downie's English wife.*[a] *Living on an allowance from her husband who is in the Spanish service*
18[4]	*Now Stamp Distributer for the County of Renfrew & Bute. Residence, Greenock*
19[5]	*Decayed manufacturer Poor Poor*
20[6]	*Decayed manufacturer, brother of above, poor poor*
21[7]	*Has extensive clothes clubs. Must have lost terribly this year by them. The father of Kevan Drummond & Kevan, Glasgow; gave his son £500 to begin that concern. A respectable man and if not gone has made money*
22	*A self-taught artist and very astonishingly takes the lead in the line*
23[8], **24**[9]	*Poor poor went through the Gazzette [sic] lately.*[b] *Disreputable*
28	*Respectable. Gave a considerable sum for property lately. Offered £3,000 for the gardens he has but was refused*

---

[a] John Downie, born 1780, with Sir John Moore at Corunna; founded and was Colonel Commandant General of the Loyal Legion of Estremadura; Knight of the Order of Merit of Charles III, 1812; Freeman of Glasgow (The Royal Military Chronicle, Vol.6, May 1813)

[b] The Gazzette in this instance is likely to have been the Edinburgh Gazette of 1837

Duncan, John, spirit dealer, 42 Millerston
Dunlop, Archibald, of Dunlop & Macfarlane—house 26 Causeyside
Dunlop, Christopher, foreman to Kerr, John and Co., 17 Abbey street—house 3 Christie street
Dunlop, Rev. David, session clerk, Abbey Parish—house Ferguslie house
Dunlop, George, cowfeeder, 3 Underwood lane
Dunlop, James, (waiter) eating house, & spirit dealer, 6 Abbey close
—Dunlop & Macfarlane, tobacconists, 2 High street
Dunlop, Peter, slademan to Saucel Brewery Company— house 7 Wardrop street
Dunlop, Ritchie, tailor, 16 Thread street
—Dunlop, Robert, grocer and spirit dealer, 95 Causeyside
Dunlop, William, grocer, 25 George street
Dunn, John, grocer, 8 Ferguslie
—Dunn, John, writer, 5 Moss street—house 42 High street
—Dunn, William, manufacturer, Barterholm
Durning, James, broker and shoemaker, 52 High street
Dyer & Co., tea & coffee dealers, 45 New street, Alex. Muir, salesman—house 24 Glen street
Dykes, James, agent, house 106 Causeyside
—Dykes, James, grocer and grain dealer, 12 Abbey close
—Dykes, Thomas, starcher, 99 Causeyside—house do.

EADIE, John, grocer & spirit dealer, 32 Broomlands
Eadie, William, pattern drawer, 58 Storie street
—Eaglesim, R. & T., cloth merchants, 105 High street
Eaglesim, Robert, of Eaglesim, R. & T.—house 3 Moss st.
Eaglesim, Thomas, of Eaglesim, R. & T.—ho. Causeyside
Eddie, William, pattern drawer, 58 Storie street
—Edmiston, Mrs. John, spirit dealer, 6 New Sneddon
—Edmiston, William, spirit dealer, 34 Canal street
Edwards, William, broker, 76 Broomlands
Elliot, Arthur, broker, 77 High street
Elliot, William, enterer, 10 Sandholes
Erskine, Alexander, cowfeeder, 40 Millerston
Erskine, James, tailor, 9 Maxwellton street
Erskine, John, mangler, 9 Maxwellton street

Entry	**Page 34**
4[1]	*Tutor to the Ferguslie family. Miser and as such has made considerable money*
7	*Macfarlane son of Hugh page 64 would be accommodated with a little money from his father. Dunlop a young journeyman in the trade not known to have anything but his abilities. One year in trade. Great dash*
10	*Has much property but being of the Old School his trade has left him. Wealthy & yearly poorer*
13[2]	*Not wealthy but has a good business, and highly respectable*
14	*Had once means but they are gone. <u>Specious loopy bodie</u> – To be as honest as <u>Willie</u> <u>Dinn</u> is a Paisley proverb*
18	*Poor*
19[3]	*Respectable well-meaning man, Church elder. No means*
22	*A bold push for a fortune. Had no money nor has made any. Bought greatly of their acquired means. Beware*
26[4]	*Miserably poor. Husband committed suicide. Kept in the shop by her brothers who all have money*
27	*Long in the line. Had a good run. Means unknown*

Erskine, Miss, dressmaker, 9 Maxwellton street
Erskine, Robert, warper, 2 Bridge street (burgh)
3 – Erskine, Thos., singeing house, 42 Causeyside—ho. 43 do.
Ewing, Thomas, Abbey church officer, 29 New Smithhills
Excise Office, 109 High street, (see public offices)

4 – FALCONER, James, pawnbroker, 134 George street—house 69 High street
5 – Falconer, John, coal agent, 61 New Sneddon—ho. 84 do.
Falconer, Rev. James, 1 Maxwellton
Falconer, William, surgeon, 6 Neilston street
6 – Fairley, George & Co., pawnbrokers, 34 Causeyside—ho. 36 do.
Fairley, James, sexton, West Relief—house 53 Canal st.
7 – Farquharson, Robert, manufacturer, 14 St. Mirren street—thread work, 8 St. James' street—house 7 St. James' place
Fergus, James, surgeon & druggist, 23 Gauze street—house 20 Orchard street
Fergus, James, sen., teacher 11 Abbey street
Fergus, James, jun., teacher, 5 Storie st.—ho. 47 High st.
8 – Fergus, John, general furnishing warehouse, 25 High st.
9 – Fergus, John, manufacturer, 25 High street
Fergus, Walter, wright, 5 Stow street
Ferguson, Daniel, smith and farrier, Lylesland
Ferguson, Daniel, spirit dealer, 32 Canal street
Ferguson, John, cowfeeder, 53 Back Sneddon
Ferguson, John, gardener, West March—shop 7 Smithhills
Ferguson, John, spirit dealer, 17 Canal street
Ferguson, Misses—house 3 New Sneddon
10 – Ferguson, Mrs. Patrick, grocer and chandler, 93 High st.
Ferguson, Peter, quarter master, Renfrewshire militia, 60 New Sneddon
11 – Ferguson & Watson, silk merchants, 14 Causeyside
Ferrie, Alexander, confectioner and spirit dealer, (Mason Lodge) 43 New street
Ferrie, Andrew, flesher and spirit dealer, 4 St. Mirren st.
Ferrie, John, flesher, 17 Sandholes
Findlater, William, Excise Officer—house 62 Causeyside
12 – Findlay, James, agent Bank of Scotland, 8 St. Mirren street, house 2 Oakshaw head

BORLAND'S FOWLER 47

Entry	**Page 35**[a]
3	*Father & sons. Hard working people have made a little property and are easy*
4[1]	*Son of an old tricky body who died in jail for forging or altering an old receipt for taxes. Was left a little money and got 4 or £500 by his wife who is dead. Strange disreputable character but not poor*
5[2]	*A brother of the same character but without a penny. Named* <u>Black Jock</u>
6[3]	*Has means. Bought a valuable property this year and has laid out some hundreds improving it. No bond. But is scarce of money and was last month (Nov) trying to borrow 2 or 300 on bill & caution*
7[4]	*Has a good business – was in 1826 hard up and oppressed. A large estate of which he was the heir of entail fell in to him about 1828*
8, 9	*A decayed manufacturer struggling for an honest sustenance for himself and family enforced to relinquish the name. Without any business but the shop. No means*
10[5]	*Very old establishment. Has means. Trade not modernised and limited*
11	*A Glasgow concern Agent here A Whitehill. Have made tremendous bad debts. Watson as McAlpine & Watson failed 1837*
12[6]	*A native of Paisley left it in 1820 Returned 1838. Had lost all knowledge of the town. Gave credit to all and sundry indiscriminately. A good natural confiding easy man. Has been in a quiet manner the cause of the great crisis in the Paisley trade. Numerous losses*

---

[a] This is the only page numbered, from entry 3, consecutively

36 PAISLEY.

1 Findlay, John, gunsmith, 37 New street
Findlay, R. B., clerk, Bank of Scotland—house 2 Oakshaw head
2 —Finlayson, J. & W., florists and seedsmen, 104 High st.
Finlayson, James, florist, house 4 Clark's place, Seedhill
Finlayson, James, tailor and habit-maker, 5 Storie street
6 —Finlayson, Wm., shawl manufacturer, 109 Causeyside
7 —Fisher, George, wright and glazier, 81 New Sneddon
Fisher, Thomas, tailor, 11 Broomlands
9 —Fleming, David, confectioner, 100 Causeyside and 46 Moss street
10 —Fleming, Gavin, builder, 89 High street
11 —Fleming, James, grocer and coal dealer, 56 Storie street
12 —Fleming, John, jun., upholsterer, 122 George street
13 —Fleming, John, upholsterer, 33 High street.—ho. 3 Albion street
Fleming, Mrs., grocer, 24 Broomlands
15 —Fleming, Wm, pawnbroker, 49 High street— ho. 53 do.
16 - Fleming, Wm., shawl manufacturer, 6 Causeyside
17 —Fletcher, Hugh, (Three Tun Tavern,) 1 High street
18 —Forbes, Chirney, & Hutchison, manufacturers, 5 Forbes place, and 6 Water brae, (burgh)
Forbes, James, jun , of Forbes, Chirney, & Hutchison—ho. Marchfield
20 —Forbes, James, sen., of Marchfield
Forbes, John, linen weaver, Rowan street
Forbes, Mrs., milliner and dressmaker, 9 Wellmeadow
23 —Forbes & Watson, grain and coal merchants, King street, Saucel
24 —Forrest, Wm., wright and timber merchant, 10 Inkle st.—house do.
Forrester, John, spirit dealer, 150 George street
Forsyth, Robt., grocer & spirit dealer, 95 New Sneddon
Fortune, Robert, spirit dealer, 94 High street
25 —Foulds, And., brass founder, 24 High st.—ho. 38 New st.
26 Foulds, Andrew, cooper, 95 High street
Foulds, Andrew, saucel distillery spirit cellar, 11 Abbey close and 4 Abbey street
31 —Foulds, Matthew, tertius, reedmaker, 1 George street—house 15 Wardrop street

Entry	Page 36
1	*Almost no business. In the old school. Always in poverty. But for the rents of a house left by his father in law, would be in misery*
3	*Enthusiasts. Helped to get up a shop by acquisition, will not succeed. December shop given up*
6[1]	*Failed. Composition 1/2. Debts £1,000*

168

7[2]	*A leader of the Volunteers. A committee man in every public management – Hospital, Infirmary &c but withal a careful man and a tolerable trade. Means very limited*
9	*Has means, both in business and lent out where a little extra interest can be got. He lost £100 with the Saracens Head this year. Cash bad*
10[3]	*Poor Got entangled with a building society last year and has several bills £1,000 and upward laying over in Glasgow Union*
11	*Has a great deal of property of the class for tradesmen which this year will yield nothing*
12	*Failed last year 1840. Cannot succeed*
13[4]	*Father of the above. A long established business the partner Baillie Spiers retired from the business some years ago and took a large sum out of it. Though not poor is not wealthy and has not been making money of late*
15[5]	*Left considerable means about 4 years ago by his father, who with his mother were suffocated in bed by charcoal fumes drying a house they had built at Largs – Must be comfortable to live*
16	*Has not failed but is known not to have made anything Last year McGilveray & Fleming Consignees to Wingate Son & Co*
17[6]	*Respectable tavern. Easy in circumstances*
18[7]	*Highly respectable. Excellent business & in undoubted credit and have means at command*
20[8]	*Father of the above reputed 20 to 25 thousand pounds. Has much valuable property Bank, Gas Water &c. Sharp*
23	*Same person as 20. D Watson junr partner manages the concern. Forbes sleeping partner*
24	*Has some good property – and a good business managed by junr partner – Hutton. Forrest very occupied*
28	*In no credit – does not deserve it*
(29)	*Dead*
31[9]	*A Chartist leader, without means and little trade*

Fowler, George, publisher, bookseller, and bookbinder, Directory office 57 Canal street
Fowler, Joseph, bookseller and stationer, 10 Gauze st.
Frame, James, grocer and spirit dealer, 3 Old Sneddon
France, Rev. William, U. S. C. 49 Oakshaw street
Fraser, Donald, at Drummond, Wm., ho. 19 Old Sneddon
Fraser, George, tailor, 78 High street
Fraser, James, grocer and tea merchant, 16 Wellmeadow —house do.
Fraser, John, boot and shoemaker, 13 Back Sneddon
Fraser, Kenneth, hair dresser, 33 Causeyside
Fraser, Peter, (George Inn and Hotel) 2 Smithhills—coaches, chaises, hearses, gigs, saddle horses, &c.
Fraser, William, spirit merchant, 106 George street
Fullarton, Alexander, copper and tinsmith, 98 High st. —house 29 Oakshaw street
Fulton, Col. Robert of Hartfield, Maxwellton house
Fulton, James, grocer and ham curer, 14 St Mirren st— house 6 Moss street
Fulton, J. & W., bleachers, scourers, and shawl washers, Glenfield
Fulton, Mrs. Wm., heddlecaster, 7 Ferguslie, East lane
Fulton, Peter, South Church officer, 9 Neilston street
Fulton, Robt., canal store keeper, 18 Canal st.—ho. 17 do.
Fulton, Robt., manager at Ross and Duncan's, 6 Abercorn street
Fulton, Robert, manufacturer, 51 Mill street
Fulton, Thos., manuf., 8 Causeyside—ho. 57 George st.
Fulton, Wm., victualler and spirit dealer, 22 Lawn st.
Futt, Mary, grocer and spirit dealer, 17 Ferguslie
Fyfe, Mrs., druggist and midwife, 29 St. James' st.

GALBREATH, Archibald, teacher, 25 Oakshaw street
Galbreath, Charles, spirit dealer, 1 Cowieston
Galbreath, Jas., (No. 2) U. S. C. church officer & sexton, 5 Abbey close
Galbreath, Mrs., straw hat maker, 5 Abbey close
Galen, John, tailor, 2 Garthland street
Gallagher, Mrs. Duncan, spirit dealer, 18 Abbey close
Galt, Hugh, turner and wheel wright, 9 New Sneddon

Entry	**Page 37**
1	*In credit, having succeeded to his father's business who has considerable means, and would get a little money when he command*
2	*Father of the above. Retired and living on his rents. The father of the trade*
7	*Old established business said to be easy in circumstances but not wealthy*
10	*Formerly of the Saracen's Head. Failed about 1826. Has since made a little money. Purchased and paid stables 2 years ago £600. Well frequented house*
12[1]	*Wealthy for his profession. Has several thousand pounds in Gas, Water, &c shares and an excellent business*
13	*Vast extent of property but considered poor for his rank. Property bonded*
14[2]	*In good credit and has some means good established business*
15	*Have some means rapidly made which must have fallen this year. Have been much involved. Still in good credit*
20[3]	*Unknown in the trade. This year's creation*
21[4]	*Wealthy – Gas, Water, Bank and Insurance Company shares. Has good property and not being able to manufacture with no profits has been almost driven from the trade*
23[5]	*Husband died 3 years ago Insolvent*
25	*Our leading teacher. Has made money. Has good property*

Galt, John, boot and shoe maker, 5 New Sneddon
Galt, John, pattern drawer, 6 Barclay street
Galt, Robert, general grocer, 2 Smithhills
Galt, Misses, 7 St. Mirren street
Gardner, Alex., printer, bookseller, and stationer, 3 Moss st.—printing office, 9 do.—house Greenhill Cottage
Gardner, Alex., spirit dealer and flesher, Earl Grey place, Lylesland
Gardner, Andrew, peruke maker and hair cutter, 12 St. Mirren street
Gardner, Archd., writer, 3 Moss st.—ho. Nethercommon
Gardner, James, feuar, 7 Smithhills
Gardner, Mrs., straw hat maker, 90 Canal street
Gardner, Robert, farmer, Underwood st. (foot of Well st.)
Gardner, Thos., cutler and edge tool maker, 31 High st.
Garvin, Mrs., broker, 9 Broomlands
Garvin, Peter, furnishing shop, 38 New street
Gavin, James, manufacturer, 3 Millerston
Gavin, John, slademan, 24 Broomlands
Geddes, Robert, victualler, 24 Wellmeadow
Gemmell, Andrew, warper, 26 Causeyside
Gemmell, J., teacher, 160 George street
Gemmell, Jas., shawl manufacturer, 116 Causeyside—ho. 16 Cotton street
Gemmell, John, carter and cowfeeder, 15 Back Sneddon
Gemmell, John, dyer, Christie lane, New Sneddon—ho. 5 do.
Gemmell, John, (Bull Inn,) 5 New street—noddies, gigs, droskies and horses to hire, carriers' quarters, and keeper of Abbey parish hearse
Gemmell, John, writer, Gilmour st.—ho. 21 Caledonia st.
Gemmell, Miss J., milliner and straw hat maker, 1 Burn row
Gemmell, Mrs., cowfeeder, 5 New Sneddon
Gemmell, Mrs., glove and hosiery shop, 5 Moss street
Gemmell, Peter, warper, 15 Causeyside
Gemmill & Smith, silk mercers and woollen drapers, 13 High street
Gemmill, Francis, of Gemmill and Smith—ho. 1 Maxwell street

Entry	**Page 38**
1	*7 years ago an industrious working man – got into note as making a first rate article. Has increased his trade greatly. In good credit but limited means. Has no shop*
5	*A respectable man – careful attention and has, for the past 7 years, apparently been doing well. Best business of the line in town, limited in means for the extent of business*
8[1]	*Heir of Nielson of Nethercommon who died last year leaving £18,000 for an academy or asylum for the destitute. Got £8,000 or £10,000 including House &c for his heirship*
9[2]	*Living on his rents. A natural son of the late A Gardner, Banker, who gave him a large House <u>in gift</u> when in his good days. rental 60 to 70 pounds. Gardner died insolvent ruined by Peruvian Bonds &c*
12[3]	*Absconded to America 3 years ago, reported drowned on the voyage. His widow on the point of marriage when he popped in one night, May last, and stopped it. A stuppid [sic] fool*
15	*Has neither credit nor means <u>nor trade</u>*
17	*A bustling trader Has paid his way for the last 7 years Came to the town at that time a stranger. Means unknown said by 24 [Robert Reid], page 75, a retired grocer, to be easy in the world – beware*
20	*Poor. Paid 1/6 in 1828 and has never got into credit. Merely a kind of agent*
23	*Failed 1837 for the 5 time and it is said did so quietly once since that date*
24[4]	*Lives genteely but no one knows where the means come from – little business*
27[5]	*Very poor well doing woman*
29	*Gemmell left means by his father who died 1835 leaving property and £1,000 insured on his life. Into a bad trade with which they are unacquainted and not likely to make by it*

Gentles, John, plumber and gas fitter, 5 Orr square
Gentles, Thomas, plumber and brass founder, 32 High street—house 44 New street
George, Adam, general washing field, 62 New Sneddon
George, John, musician, 22 Lawn street
Gibb, Alexander, of Gibb & Thomson—house Linside
—Gibb, George, writer, 6 Moss street—ho. 32 Calside
—Gibb, James, (Commercial Inn and Coffee House) 51 Moss street, and 103 High street (Cross)
Gibb, Matthew, paver, 11 Glen street
Gibb, Mrs. John, 32 Calside
Gibb, Thomas, Martyrs' church officer and sexton—ho. 7 West Campbell street
—Gibb, Robert, joiner and cart wright, 3 Mill street
—Gibb & Thomson, bleachers, Linside
Gibb, William, flower-lasher, 83 Causeyside
—Gibb, William, late merchant, 11 St. James' place
Gibson, Alexander, furnishing shop, 16 Wellmeadow
Gibson, A., grocer, 23 Oakshaw street
—Gibson, Alexander, manufacturer, 8 Moss street
—Gibson, A., writer, and Justice of Peace clerk depute, County Buildings—house 44 High street
Gibson, Allan, clothlapper, 113 Causeyside
Gibson, Andrew, cork manufacturer, 13 High street
Gibson, Andrew, flower-lasher, 143 George street
Gibson, Andrew, of Gibson, J. & A.—house 6 Gauze st.
Gibson, Andrew, spirit dealer, 38 Moss street
— Gibson and Barclay, bakers, 30 High street
— Gibson and Craig, wine, spirit, and tea merchants, 107 and 108 High street
Gibson, Francis, spinning master, Underwood mill
Gibson, James, baker, 38 High street
Gibson, James, spirit dealer, 41 Ferguslie
Gibson, John, of Gibson, J. & A., house 8 Moss street
Gibson, John, spirit dealer, 7 Ferguslie
—Gibson, J. & A., yarn merchants, 113 Causeyside
Gibson, Miss—house 44 High street
Gibson, Mrs. N.—house 44 High street
Gibson, William, of Gibson & Craig—ho. 42 Oakshaw st.
—Giffen, William—house Canal bank

Entry	**Page 39**
1	*No means. Left the town*
2	*Sequestrated. Had an excellent opportunity of succeeding but foolishly speculating in large Railway &c stock ruined himself*
6	*No means. The working member of McPherson, Caldwell & Gibb from whom he has separated. Is respectable and diligent*
7[1]	*Has done well. House not of the quietest kind but pays well. 7 years ago purchased the tavern he occupies and since that time some other property in town*
11	*Insolvent*
12	*Insolvent. Composition 4/6*
14	*Liferenter in property left by Nielson of Nethercommon – married to his niece*
17	*Should not have a place in Directory has no trade nor money*
18[2]	*Can with great difficulty get day and way. Supports a mother and sisters in a genteel way. His father and grandfather were town clerks in their day and lived at or above their income*
24	*No means and but little trade, were journeymen bakers lately to Baking Association*
25[3]	*Succeeded about 1828 to Mrs Hamilton's trade on her retiring from business, being her shopmen. Are in good credit and have certainly done well. Have an excellent business*
31	*30 years in business. Have suffered hugely by bad debts. Are not doubted but cannot have great means at command*
35[4]	*Late canal manager retired on a small reversion, Means limited*

Gilchrist, Allan, boot and shoemaker, 8 New street
Gilchrist, John, silk, cotton, and woollen dyer, Blackhall Dyeworks— ho. do.—receiving office, 24 Orchard st.
Gilchrist, Andrew, precentor, Martyrs' church—house 78 George street
—Gillespie, James, spirit dealer and eating house, 22 Smithhills
Gillespie, John, of Campbell & Gillespie—house 59 Love street
—Gillespie, William, slater and slate merchant, 43 Moss street—slate yard, 82 New Sneddon
—Gillies, Alexander, manufacturer, 150 George street
—Gillies, David, baker, 100 Causeyside
Gillin, Andrew, porter, 5 St. Mirren street
Gillin, Charles, porter, 106 Causeyside
Gillin, Patrick, porter, 3 Storie street
—Gilmour, A., wine and spirit merchant, 102 High street —house 31 Gauze street
Gilmour, Archibald—house 56 Causeyside
Gilmour & Co., booksellers and stationers, 20 Causeyside
Gilmour, Hugh, flesher, 1 Ferguslie
Gilmour, James, cowfeeder, 23 Glen street
Gilmour, John, house 56 Causeyside
—Gilmour, John, land surveyor, 2 Espedair street
Gilmour, Mrs. And., grocer and cowfeeder, 134 George st.
—Gilmour, Mrs. James, spirit dealer, 24 New street
—Gilmour, Mrs. Matthew, (King's Arms Inn,) carriers' quarters, 25 High street
—Gilmour, Peter, wright and window glazier, 4 Lawn st.
—Gilmour Street boot and shoe shop, Gilmour street
—Gilmour, Thomas & Co., silk and shawl merchants, 2 Forbes' place
—Gilmour, Thos., of Gilmour, Thos. & Co.—ho. Prospect hill
Gilroy, Miss, straw hat maker, Lylesland
Gilroy, Mrs., grocer, Lylesland
Glasgow and Paisley Joint Railway Parcel Office, 2 Causeyside, John Lawson, manager—ho. 6 Stow st.
—Glassford, David, silk dyer and renovator, 10 St. Mirren street— dyeworks, 29 Causeyside

Entry	**Page 40**
2	*Sequestrated composition 3/- <u>4th time</u>*
4	*Disreputable house. Dangerous character. Has been in Bridewell for stabbing cartmen, goes by the cognomen of the "Fly"*
6	*Succeeded lately to his father's trade which is respectable. Has some property left him. Is a well doing journeyman*
7	*Absconded*
8[1]	*Insolvent. Dissipated character*
12[2]	*Good appearance in trade which was left by his father. Old established business 50 years standing. Is known at times to be "<u>Hard life</u>" and has been so for the last 12 years*
18[3]	*Great parts but never sober*
20	*Her husband a decayed manufacturer at his last shift. Poor widow*
21	*A poor widow. Insolvent at her husband's death 2 years ago*
22	*Had once much valuable property now all gone. In misery*
23[4]	*A dash that must be carefully avoided. See P Murdoch & Son*
24[5]	*Insolvent paid 13/- 1841*
25[6]	*[Blank]*
29	*A jobbing renovator without means*

Gleed, John S., excise officer, house 3 Lonend
Glen, Allan, tailor, 89 Causeyside
3 —Glen, Anderson, & Co., thread manufs. 34 Gordon's lane
4 —Glen, H., tuscan and straw hat manufacturer, 86 High st.
Glen, Hugh, of Glen, Anderson, & Co.—ho. 86 High st.
Glen, James, farmer, Hawkhead Mains
7 —Glen, Thomas, grain merchant and miller, Hawkhead mills—and baker, 18 Broomlands
1 —Glen, Walter, cloth merchant, 12 George street
Glendinning, Thos., basket maker, 36 St. James' st.
Gold, James, tailor, 16 Storie street
Gold,-Mrs., mangler, 13 New street
Goldie, Henry, tailor, 23 Wellmeadow
Gollan, Dan., crystal and stoneware merch. 8 Broomlands
Goodlet, Thomas, comic singer, 3 Bridge street (burgh)
Goudie, Wm., cooper and riddle maker, 48 & 49 High st.
Goudielock, William, clothlapper, 8 Forbes' place
17 —Gowans, Thomas, gardener, Orr Town
Graham, Alex., brewer, Saucel brewery Co., 9 Saucel—house do.
19 —Graham, Andrew, tea dealer, 99 Causeyside
Graham, James, spirit dealer, 105 George street
Graham, John, wine and spirit merchant, 1 Old Sneddon
Graham, Mrs. Edward & Co., new clothing shop 1 St. Mirren street
Graham, Neil, cooper, 10 Moss street
Graham, Rev. James, 21 St. James' street
Graham, Robert, manager, Saucel distillery, King street, Saucel—house 3 Bladda
Graham, Thomas, clothier, 47 Moss street—draper and clothier, 14 St. Mirren street—ho. do.
27 —Graham, Thomas, wine and spirit merchant, 88 High st.
Granger, Luke, tailor, 15 Back row, Sandholes
Granger, Mrs., eating house, 9 Broomlands
30 —Grant, Gershom, clerk, Western Bank, 1 Forbes' place—ho, 12 Saucel
31 —Grant, James, collector of Police assessments, office County Buildings—house 10 Abbey street
Gray, David & John, wood turners, 4 Storie street
Gray, Mrs., teacher of music, 16 Storie street

D 2

Entry	**Page 41**
3[1]	*Means not well known but are seen not to be rich. Are in good credit and reckoned safe*
4	*Senior partner of the above concern. Once with a splendid shop, the business carried now by the family under the husband's name as formerly*
7	*Has acquired considerable means. Had a credit account with the Paisley Bank of £500 till 1830 when one of his cautioners died. Was deeply involved in the grain speculation, the Bank got alarmed, called up the money which he paid and went angrily with his account to the Paisley Union. He now acknowledges that the check saved him from ruin as he could not speculate in 1832 the bad year*
8	*Nicknamed "Confusion", Has not paid a bill without expenses these 20 years. Reduced from a Dashy shop to a mere kitchen trade. No credit*
17	*Has tried many shifts, but now a poor labouring gardener*
19	*Disreputable character. Made money prior to 1820 tried to fail about 1826 but was made to pay. Returned from America 1832 and got a little credit as a manufacturer. Tried to fail again by secreting money in some bank in Glasgow. It was taken from him. He was forced out of trade. Now a tea hawker*
27	*Very wealthy. Much property, Gas, Water, Bank &c shares*
30	*[Blank]*
31	*Has several Bank shares and money in Western – and half pay*

Gray, Robert, St. Mirren street tavern, 5 St. Mirren st.
Gray, William, spirit dealer, 66 Causeyside
Gray, William, spirit dealer, 11 St. Mirren street
Greenfield, John, excise officer—house 5 Caledonia st.
Greenlees, Hugh, manufacturer, 112 Causeyside
Greenlees, Matthew, manufacturer, 14 Causeyside—ho. Cartvale
Greenlees, Mrs., stay maker, 94 High street
Greenlees, Thomas, of Greenlees, Thomas & Co.—ho. 56 Canal street
Greenlees, Thomas & Co., silk merchants, 13 Causeyside
Greer and Steele, shawl manufacturers, 6 Causeyside
Grieve, Macgregor, & Co., silk gauze manufacturers, 26 Orchard street
Grieve, Lieut. George, Blackhall
Guthrie, David F., furniture warehouse, 34 High street —workshop, 101 Causeyside
Guthrie, James, shawl commission agent, 16 Causeyside
Guthrie, Mrs., William, milliner and straw hat maker, 26 Gauze street
Guthrie, Robert, & Co., manufacturers, 4 Causeyside
Guthrie, William, of Morton, John & Co.—house 10 Barclay street
Guy, Walter, cooper, 49 High street

HAIR, John, manufacturer, 15 Causeyside—ho. 56 do.
Halden, George, warper, 109, Causeyside—house 7 Wellmeadow
Halden, John & Co., manufacturers, 9 Marshall's lane
Halden, John, of Halden, John, & Co.—house Camphill
Halden, Mrs., leghorn & straw hat maker, 7 Wellmeadow
Hall, John, gardener and fruit shop, 17 Back Sneddon
Hamilton, Adam, of Lounsdale
Hamilton, Adam, & Sons, bleachers, Blackland mill
Hamilton, Alex.—house Blackland mill
Hamilton, Alex., teacher of drawing, 18 Orchard street
Hamilton, Alex., victualler & spirit dealer, 67 Causeyside
Hamilton, Elizabeth, furnishing shop, 34 Wellmeadow
Hamilton, George, manager Blackland mill
Hamilton, Hugh, builder and contractor, 15 Sir Michael st.

Entry	**Page 42**
1	*An industrious man. Foreman to William Carlile & Co. Respectable house kept by the wife. In good credit and likely to do well*
5[1]	*[Blank]*
6	*Insolvent debts £13,900. Composition 11/- ruined by the foolish speculations of a brother in London*
9	*Insolvent. Debts £ [blank], Comp [blank]. Brother of 6 [Matthew] and involved in same ruin*
10	*Insolvent debts £6,500. Composition 1/11*
11	*Have considerable means, cannot make with a profit and match competition, and are doing nothing*
14	*Of doubtful fame and credit*
16	*William McAlister (see Western shareholders) the sleeping partner which makes the company good. The writer of this asked the company's signature and got it from William McAlister*
18[2]	*Has suffered by the crisis this year and though scarce of means, and sometimes embarrassed is supposed to get on*
19[3]	*Wealthy. Had about 1822 £1,000 left him in South America and in 1831 £3,000 by a brother. Does a small business*
21[4]	*Insolvent debts £11,000. Composition 7/6*
25[5]	*Wealthy bleacher retired*
26	*D[itt]o [Wealthy bleacher]. Brother of 25 in a good business*
27	*[This may be the brother to which entry 26 refers.]*
29	*Poor industrious and careful but no means*
32[6]	*Is said to have made a little money perhaps 2 or 3 hundred pounds*

Hamilton, James, clothier, habit and pelisse maker, 65 Love street
Hamilton, James, coal agent, King street, Saucel—house 8 Lonend
Hamilton, James, spirit dealer, 65 Love street
Hamilton, John—house Blackland mill
Hamilton, John, baker, 103 Causeyside
Hamilton, John, boot and shoemaker, 9 School wynd
Hamilton, John, foreman at M'Kechnie, Kerr, & Co.—house 34 Wellmeadow
Hamilton, John, grocer, 44 Broomlands
Hamilton, Jn., precentor, West Relief—ho. 32 Broomlands
Hamilton, John, writer, 4 Moss st.—ho. 140 George st.
Hamilton, Miss, furnished lodgings, 10 Barclay street
Hamilton, Mrs, 22 Moss street
Hamilton, Thomas, hosier, 43 High street
Hamilton, William, bleacher, Lounsdale
Handel, Robert, gardener, 4 Wellmeadow
Hanna, David, grocer, 29 Glen street
Hanna, Robert, of Reid & Hanna—house 8 George st.
Hannah, George, cowfeeder, 13 Newton street
Hannah, James, broker, 28 New Smithhills
Hannah, James, pattern drawer, 9 Gauze street
Hannay, William, silver smith and jeweller, 19 Hight st.—house Burns' place
Hardie, Mrs. William, Burns' place
Hardie, William, shoemaker, Williamsburgh
Harkness, William, teacher, Paisley Educational Association, school 64 Causeyside
Harper, Andrew, sheriff officer, 32 Gauze street
Harper, James, spirit dealer, 26 South Croft street—ho. 10 Wallneuk
Harper, Robert, shoemaker, 39 Stock street
Harris, Alexander, watch and clock maker, 25 High st.
Harrison, James, contractor, Underwood street
Harrow, Wilson, & Co., calico, woollen, and silk printers, Collinslee—residence, Wester Carriagehill place
Hart, John, clerk post office—house Christie street
Hart, John, draper, general furnishing shop, 101 High street—house Cartvale

Entry	**Page 43**
1	*Has some well rented property, bonded, but must be worth a little money. Had £300 1828 when he built the property*
10[1]	*Clever but dissipated. Himself or family will have considerable means at his mother's death No.12 [Mrs Hamilton]*
12	*[Blank]*
14[2]	*Has considerable means, and a good business succeeded to when his father retired. A sporting gentleman*
21[3]	*Has the principal trade of the kind in Paisley. Has been 40 years in business. Is supposed to have considerable means. Has some good house property*
26	*Poor*
30	*Company commenced in 1833 by 11 printers who were put out of work from being concerned in a strike. Have done well. Are in good credit and have made a little money*
32	*Wealthy and has a good business proprietor of Cartvale House which cost £1,000 Highly respectable*

Hart, John, painter and precentor, Underwood street
Hart, John, writer, 87 High street, and 9 Church hill—house 87 High street
Hart, Miss Jane, dress-maker, 63 George street
Hart, Mrs., grocer, 4, Storie street
Hart, Mrs. Robert, spirit dealer, (Vine Inn,) 21 Smithhills
Hart, Robert, farmer, Pennelly
Hart, Robert, grocer, 2 Well street
Hart, Thomas, grocer and spirit dealer, 11 Williamsburgh
Hart, William, (Swan Inn,) 22 New Smithhills
Hart, William, writer, auctioneer, and appraiser, 13 Old Sneddon
Harvey, Brand, & Co., silk throwsters, Blackhall factory—orders received at 107 Causeyside
Harvey, J. & Co., wine and spirit merchants, King street, Saucel
Harvey, James, of Harvey, James & Co.—ho. 8 Saucel
Harvey, John, smith, and spirit dealer, 3 Mile house
Harvie, James, turner, 39 High street
Hastie, Archibald, baker, 4 Lawn street
Hastie, Archibald, Esq., M.P. for Paisley, residence Finsbury Square, London
Hatrick, Alexander, smith, bell hanger, and gas fitter, 21 High street
Hatrick, Matthew, lead drawer, 48 Causeyside
Hatrick, William, wholesale and retail genuine drug and patent medicine warehouse, 4 High st —ho. 54 do.
Hay, Charles, railway tavern, 13 Moss street
Hay, John, of Hay, Robert & Son—house 77 Canal st.
Hay, Peter, silk dyer and renovator, 33 Gauze street—house do.
Hay, Robert & Son, engravers, copperplate printers, and lithographers, 15 St. Mirren street, and 7 Abbey street
Hay, Robert, of Hay, Robert & Son—house 77 Canal st.
Hector, Misses, milliners and dressmakers, 46 Moss st.
Hedley, William, excise officer—house Glen street
Hegney, Arthur, surgeon and druggist, 25 Old Sneddon
Henderson, A. P., writer, 87 High street

Entry	**Page 44**
2[1]	*Has an excellent business. Inattentive and always in confusion. Wealthy but always in want of money. 29 of this page [A P Henderson] brought from Starvation in Edinburgh to bring up arrears of business which are immense*
5	*Not respectable House not reputable attended by genteel loose company. Of doubtful means*
8	*Long in the line but not supposed to have made any thing by it*
10	*Poor. Might do well but never sober*
11	*Of Glasgow. And understood here to be very wealthy. Make a dreadful amount of bad debts in Paisley*
12	*First trade of the town in the line. Supposed to be wealthy. Large business*
16	*Bankrupt in 1818 and 1835. Poor*
18	*Poor a mere jobber*
20	*From Apothecary Hall Glasgow about 7 years ago. Reduced the price of drugs in Paisley 50 percent. Has secured an excellent trade. Is said to have made a little money and it would seem so from the purchases he is known to make as an importer*
23[2]	*Merely a clothes cleaner of no repute*
24	*Are easy and have a first rate business. Have house property free. Half proprietor of the Paisley Advertiser which is now valuable*
28	*Poor and dissipated*
29	*See 2 [John Hart] above. Jeeringly spoke of under the cognomen of Wee Peerie*

—Henderson, Andrew, baker, 12 Gauze street
—Henderson, John, cutler and hardware merchant, 19 High street—house Camphill
—Henderson, John, spirit dealer, 12 Gauze street
Henderson, Peter, of Reid & Henderson—house 22 St. James' street
Henderson, Robert, farmer, Carriagehill house
—Henderson, Thomas, accountant, and treasurer Abbey parish poor's funds, 9 Gauze street—house 1 Great Hamilton street
Henderson, Wm., grocer, and spirit dealer, 71 Broomlands
—Henderson, William, spirit merchant, and confectioner, 22 High street—house do.
Hendry, James, feuar—house 12 Causeyside
—Hendry, O., surgeon and druggist, 15 Broomlands, and 56 George street—house do.
—Hendry, R. apothecary, 5 High street
—Hendry, Robert, grocer, 63 Causeyside
Henning, Misses, dressmakers, 89 High street
Henrie, C., teacher, 9 Ferguslie Mid lane—ho. 36 Ferguslie
Henry, John, apothecary and druggist, 82 High st—house 43 do.
Hill, Andrew, saddler, 44 New street—ho. 7 Orchard st.
—Hill, John, gardener and cowfeeder, Nethercommon
—Hill, John, gardener and fruit shop, 17 Back Sneddon
Hill, Thomas, excise officer—ho. 1 Garthland street
—Hodge, Arch., accountant, 4 Christie Terrace—ho. 61 Love street
—Hodge, J. & T., tobacconists, 20 High st.—house do.
—Hodge & Mavitie, writers, 5 Moss street
Hodge, Mrs. James—house 56 High street
Hodge, Wm., of Hodge & Mavitie—house 5 Christie st.
—Hodgert, Ninian, agent for the North British Insurance, 25 Gauze street
Hogg, John, farmer, Cardonald
Hogg, Mrs. James, spirit dealer, 27 New Sneddon
Holmes, Cunningham, spirit dealer, 38 High street
—Holms, A. C.—house Sandyford
—Holms, A. C. & Co., manufacturers, 4 Orchard street
—Holms, Alex., victualler, 6 Moss st. and 20 Broomlands

Entry	**Page 45**
1, 3	*[Andrew and John] Sporting characters. Bankrupts several times. Dangerous*
2[1]	*Provost of the Town. Had to fly to America in 1819 for Radicalism or pike making. Returned in 1821. Borrowed £60 on cautionary of friends and paid it from savings in 1826. In 1831 bought property in High street at £540 paid £240-£300 remains on old bond. Is joint proprietor and editor of the Glasgow Evening Post which publishes a Paisley department. Is a plodding character without education, of coarse manners. Has a good trade. Making his politics pay him, and is making money*
6	*Insolvent in 1836 and was so fortunate as to obtain the situation he holds*
8	*Failed as a manufacturer in 1819 in a triffling amount. Apparently doing well. His wife the daughter of an old confectioner in town, and knows her business*
10[2]	*Of no means, but what as supplied by his father No.12 [Robert]*
11[3]	*Wealthy. House property, Gas, Water &c shares. A director of most of the Public Companies*
12[4]	*In easy circumstances. Good house property and a good trade*
17, 18	*[John and John] Has some property, bonded, in straitened circumstances*
20[5]	*Industrious. Is getting on to good business. Cashier of Savings Bank*
21[6], 22, 23	*In easy circumstances, considerable means left by their father, part of which is locked up in life rent by 23 [Mrs James Hodge]. £500 given to each to commence with*
25[7]	*For 40 years teller in P U Bank now living on his means, which are considerable*
29[8]	*Wealthy*
30	*Has no existence. Warehouse merely kept as a place of call when in town*
31	*Easy. Has some money and a good business*

Holmes, James, cowfeeder, 8 Storie street
—Holms, James, manufacturer, 7 St. Mirren street—ho. Saucel Bank House
—Holms, James, spirit dealer, 10 Storie street
Holms, John, brass founder, 13 High street—house 12 Abbey street
—Holms, John, tobacconist, 100 Causeyside—house 130 George street
—Holms, Matthew, engineer, 9 Orchard street
—Holms, Matthew, joiner, 130 George street—ho. do.
Holms, Mrs., furnishing shop, 15 Smithhills
Holms, Mrs. Jas., grocer & spirit dealer, 72 Broomlands
Holms, Mrs. Janet, grocer, 60 George street
Honeyman, Miss, milliner & dressmaker, 6 Brown's lane
—Hood, Charles, (Turf Inn,) 8 Orchard street
Hood, John, brazier, tin and copper plate worker and gas fitter, 1 Smithhills—workshop, 20 do.
—Hood, John, victualler & spirit dealer, 95 New Sneddon
Hood, Thomas, grocer & victualler, 17 Lawn street
—Hope, James, auctioneer, appraiser, and general agent — house 85 New Sneddon
Hope, James, shoemaker and broker, 38 Moss street
—Hope, John L., auctioneer and appraiser, 10 Abercorn st.
—Hope, Robert, wine and spirit merchant, 12 Dyer's wynd
—Hossack, John & Co., ale & spirit merchants, 37 High st.
House of Recovery, 11 Bridge street
Houston, George, at Rowat, Robt.—ho. 45 Oakshaw st.
—Houston, James, draper, 19 High street
—Houston, John, general furnishing warehouse, 15 High street—house 97 do.
Houston, John, printcutter, at Buchanan, Walter, & Co's, Blackland mill
Houston, Mrs. George, 45 Oakshaw street
—Houston, Robert, glass, china, and stoneware merchant, 2 Smithhills—house do.
Houston, W. L., sheriff clerk depute, County Buildings, —house 34 Glen street
Howe, Mrs., furnished lodgings, 8 Abercorn street
Howie, James, cowfeeder, 5 Prussia street
Howie, Mrs., mangler, 11 Gauze street

Entry	**Page 46**
2[1]	*Of considerable means. Much good property of the best kind, and an excellent trade rather out of the common run*
3	*Without means. Small business. And presumed to be an agent for Aqua*
5	*An upstart. Means unknown – beware*
6	*Insolvent. Estate will not pay 6d per £. Company Holms & Andrew*
7[2]	*Has respectable lands of good property bonded to G F society[a] for £350 about half value. Has a fair trade not of the large speculation kind*
12	*Formerly a china merchant in town. Has been out of town 10 years. Means not well known but must be limited. Has a bad chance in his present house. Its fame left it with its former landlord (Lyall), the 2 last did no good*
14	*Disreputable*
16	*An old man who has had many ups and downs, failed in 1827 and has not got on since. Was in his day the best putter, leaper and fencer*
18-19	*Sons of the above [presumably 16] endeavouring to make their way. As to sporting they are a <u>chip of the old block. Beware</u>*
20	*Unknown in Paisley. A large dash splendidly got up last May. Has no chance of succeeding*
23, 24	*Father and son. Father failed in 1828. Well doing honest family without means and very limited credit. Small trade*
27	*Commenced 1834 with means unknown and a poor appearance of stock. Has increased his appearance wonderfully of late. Is very industrious but at all times short of funds*

---

[a] 'G F Society' may be Good Fellows Society

Howie, Robert, flesher, 16 George street
Howieson, John, agent, Skaterigg Coal Co., Harbour lane—ho. 3 Back Sneddon
Hudson, Rev. Joseph, 3 Wardrop street
Hume, Robert, grocer, 3 School wynd
Hunter, James, chimney sweep, 94 High street
Hunter, John, clerk at Barr & M'Nab's, 15 North Croft st.
Hunter, John & Co., joiners and cabinet makers, 100 High street, furniture warehouse, do.—timber yard 4 and 5 Hunter street
Hunter, John, of Hunter, John & Co.—house 101 High street
Hunter, John, spirit dealer, 20 Castle street
Hunter, John, tailor, 58 George street
Hunter, Joseph, grocer, 2 West Campbell street
Hunter, Miss, milliner and dressmaker, 44 New street
Hunter, Miss, milliner and dressmaker, 1 South Croft st.
Hunter, Richard, cowfeeder, 11 Maxwellton
Hunter, Robert, gardener, Greenlaw
Hunter, Robert, of Hunter, John & Co.—house 19 School wynd
Hunter, Thomas, spirit dealer, Fauldheads road
Hunter, Wm., cabinet maker, joiner, and weavers' wright, 84 George street
Hunter, William, druggist, 67 Causeyside
Hunter, Wm., A.M., LL.D., rector of grammar school, 5 Church hill—house do.
Hunter, Wm., tobacconist, 101 High st.—ho. 63 Love st.
Hutcheson, Mrs., grocer, stoneware and crystal shop, 28 Wellmeadow (post office receiving box)
Hutchison, Archibald, of Forbes, Chirney, & Hutchison—house 6 Stow street
Hutchison, David, dyer, 56 Causeyside—ho. 58 do.
Hutchison, James, spirit dealer, 1 St. James' street
Hutchison, James, plasterer, 3 Glen street
Hutchison, James, surgeon & druggist, 23 Causeyside—house do.
Hutchison, John, plasterer, Glen lane cottage
Hutchison, John, plasterer, 2 West street
Hutchison, Mrs. Matthew, feuar, 18 Abbey close

Entry	**Page 47**
7	*An old established house. Is very wealthy both acquired and bequeathed. Would not conform to modern law [of] property and lost their trade almost entirely 1837 but now redeemed by son No.16 [Robert] below*
16[1]	*Son of No.7 [John] above*
20	*The Doctor leaving Paisley having got the appointment of Head Master of Liverpool Academy. If he had any thing when he came to Paisley 1831 it must be gone. Poor apparently*
21	*Has means, good business and extension creating scarcity of money at times, in good credit. Son of John above*
24	*Of the lowest dissipated caste. Poor*
25	*[Blank but probably with 26-29 below]*
26[2], 27, 28[3], 29[4]	*[James, James, John and John] A well doing family who all are getting on in the world and have acquired means. Were left a few hundred pounds each by their father in 1822 and have improved the legacy. John wealthy*

48   PAISLEY.

Hutton, Arthur, foreman at Baird & Wallace—house 4 Meeting house lane
2 —Hutton, Jas. & Co., tanners & leather merchants, 4 High street
3 —Hutton, John, foreman at Forrest, Wm., 10 Inkle street—ho. 19 Thread street
Hyde, John, Blackhall factory
Hyndman, Samuel, teacher, 2 Glen street
Hyndman, Thomas, flesher and ham curer, 14 Smithhills

INGLIS, James, precentor, High church, 4 Wardrop street—teacher of music and pianoforte tuner—class room, 4 Smithhills
Ingram, James, of Ingram, Thomas & Co.—house 70 Causeyside
9 — Ingram, Thos. & Co., shawl manufs., 25 Orchard street
Ingram, Thos., of Ingram, Thos. & Co.—ho. 1 Greenlaw st
11 — Irvine, Andrew, joiner and cartwright, 1 Calside—house 15 Stevenson street.

12 — JAAP, John, boot and shoemaker, 1 High st.—ho. 2 do.
Jack, Alex., block cutter, at M'Kechnie, Kerr & Co.—house 2 Barr street
14 —Jack, John, grocer and grain merchant, 52 Storie street
15 —Jack, Peter, grocer and grain merchant, 95 High street
16 —Jack, Peter, writer, 9 Moss street—ho. 50 Love street
17 —Jack, Robert, grocer, 9 Stock street
18 —Jack, Robert, thread manuf., Cumberland factory, Laigh Kirk lane—house 36 Causeyside
Jackson, John, cowfeeder, 39 High st.
Jackson, Matthew, farmer, Rylees
Jackson, Miss, dressmaker, 39 High street
22 — Jaffray, Jas., wright and shuttle maker, 118 George st. *Poor*
23 — Jamieson, Archibald, 4 Garthland place *Wealthy*
24 — Jamieson, James, silk mercer, haberdasher, and straw hat manufacturer, 97 High street—house 46 New street
Jamieson, John, spirit dealer, fish and bacon store, 19 Smithhills
26 — Jamieson, John, manufacturer, 6 Causeyside—house 1 Maxwell street

Entry	**Page 48**
2[1]	*Bankrupt every two or three years – has easily had a scare these last 5 years. In no credit*
3	*Partner of William Forrest. Firm, Forrest & Hutton*
9[2]	*Paid 5/- in 1829. 4/- in 1841*
11	*No means. No trade*
12[3]	*Miserably poor 4 or 5 years ago. Had his furniture sequestrated for rent. Has made it better but still in very doubtful circumstances, and limited credit. Industrious.*
14[4]	*Has much valuable property. But trade gone. Would not conform to modern customs. Lost a process in House of Lords 1839 in an ill-natured case about <u>drop</u> from a neighbouring property. Expenses £15 a day*
15[5]	*Brother of 14 [John]. Very easy circumstances, good business, got a considerable sum by his wife 1839*
16[6]	*Poor. Bankrupt in 1828 as a builder, a tricky lawyer of a character to be avoided*
17	*A respectable old man of limited means*
18[7]	*Has some valuable property bonded of which it was said at the time 1836 that he paid £1,500, Does but a small trade. Has suffered considerably this year*
22[8]	*Poor*
23[9]	*Wealthy*
24	*Insolvent. Composition 10/-*
26	*Insolvent under trust. Dissipated £6,000 left him by his father all gone*

Jamieson, John, porter, Paisley Commercial Bank—ho. 4 Smithhills.
Jamieson, Miss, dressmaker, 32 High street
Jamieson, Miss, 1 Maxwell street
Jamieson, Mrs., straw hat maker, 5 Wellmeadow
Jamieson, Robert, baker, 1 Wellmeadow
Jamieson, Robert, surgeon, 68 High street
Jamieson, Robert, tailor, 9 Old Sneddon
Jamieson, William—house 97 Causeyside
Jamieson, William, grocer and spirit dealer, 18 Lawn st.
Jardine, Mrs. James, tea dealer, 56 Storie street
Jardine, R., teacher of English, writing, and arithmetic—house 49 do.
Jarvie, James, calico printer, 66 High street
Jeffrey, Alexander, grocer and spirit dealer, 3 Espedair st.
Jeffrey, William, M. D., 18 Orchard street
Johnson, Mrs. Robert, broker, 73 High street
Johnston, James, broker, 17 Moss street
Johnston, Jas., broker and weavers' office, 100 George st.
Johnston, James, flesher, 99 Causeyside—house 22 do.
Johnston, John, yarn warehouse, 6 Causeyside
Johnston, Joseph, muslin manufacturer, 18 Causeyside—house Woodside
Johnston, William, precentor, U. S. C. (No 4)—house 3 Maxwell street
Johnston, William, tailor, 103 High street
Johnston, William, teacher Infant School, 12 Lawn st.

KANE, Mrs. Hugh, broker, 23 New Smithhills
Keir, Adam, 5, Gauze street
Keir, Samuel, hairdresser, 149 George street
Keith, Alex., of Keith, Alex. & Co.—ho. 5, Garthland st.
Keith, Alexander, & Co., silk gauze manufacturers, 4 Shuttle street
Keith, James, fishmonger, 57 High street
Keith, Neil, at Lowndes, Wm., & Jas., & Co.—ho. 79 New Sneddon
Kelly, Andrew—house 9 Marshall's lane
Kelly, Peter, spirit dealer, Gilmour street—house do.

E

Entry	**Page 49**
8	*Long Jamieson & Robertson – Brother of 23 [Archibald] former page. Provost in 1816. Decayed manufacturer with a small reversion of rents. Highly respectable, and wealthy connexions*
14[1]	*Of good parts. Always in poverty supported principally on annuity of imbecile brother in law who boards with him*
18	*The most respectable in his line in the town. Has a good trade and some means*
19[2]	*Has nothing. Branched off from 20 [Josep]h before he failed to secure some agency which he held*
20[3]	*Insolvent pays 5/-*
28	*Is a brother of Keith salesman and partner (to a small extent) of Wilson & Sons, London. Concern got up 1831 or '32 as masters for that house. Had no means and will to a certainty at this time (1841) go down. A blustering foolish fellow*
32	*Came to the town about 1831. A Butler out of place. Had two or three hundred pounds. Seems to have got a tolerable business*

Kennedy, C. John, teacher—Academy, 30 Causeyside—house do.
Kennedy, David, teacher, 24 Glen street—house 5 Caledonia street
Kennedy, Hugh, carter, 67 High street
Kennedy, John, bookseller, 1 Wellmeadow
Kennedy, Mrs., dressmaker, 14 Cotton street
Kent, James, cowfeeder and grocer, 3 Cross street
—Kerr, Alex., & Co., shawl warehouse, 6 Causeyside
Kerr, David, of Kerr & Gibson—house 11 West Croft st.
—Kerr, Dr. James, and Son, 7 Orr square
—Kerr & Gibson, manufacturers, 113 Causeyside
Kerr, Hugh, agent, spirit cellar, 4 Lillias' wynd
—Kerr, James, baker, 99 High street
—Kerr, James, grocer and spirit dealer, 68 George street
Kerr, James, M.D.—house 7 Orr Square
Kerr, James, weavers' office, 84 Causeyside
—Kerr, John, baker, 94 Causeyside
—Kerr, John, & Co., manufs., 17 Abbey st.—house do.
Kerr, John, joiner and cabinet maker, 65 High street
Kerr, John, jun., of M Kechnie, Kerr, & Co.—house 94 Causeyside
—Kerr, John, & Sons, thread manufs., 28 Gordon's lane
—Kerr, John, thibet cropper and shawl cutter, 28 Gordon's lane—house 25 do.
Kerr, Mrs. Andrew, grocer, 7 Cotton street.
Kerr, Mrs. Duncan, cowfeeder, 10 Niddry street
Kerr, Mrs. Hugh, wine and spirit dealer, 7 Glen street
Kerr, Mrs. Thomas, 1 Christie street
—Kerr, Peter, and Son, heddle twine and thread manufs, 34 New street—house do.
Kerr, Robert, Black Bull tavern, 1 Dyer's wynd
—Kerr, Robert, manufacturer, 21 Thread street—house 20 do.—dyework Bladda
—Kerr, Robert, merchant and agent for Caledonian Insurance Co.—house 1 Oakshaw head
Kerr, Samuel, hair dresser, 30 Wellmeadow
Kerr, Thomas, letter runner—house 25 Cotton street
—Kerr, Thomas, thread manufacturer, 24 Glen street
Kerr, William, broker, 26 Lawn street

Entry	**Page 50**
1[1]	*A leader of the Volunteers, and forward in every foolish question that agitates the town. His family has some property which by the term of the will he is instructed to spend on them, and is supposed to be doing so. Preacher to a section of the Methodists Had once a great school which is gone from him*
7	*Only two years in existence. The partner sold property in Kilbarchan for which it is said £800 was got and which formed the capital of the company. A small sum for their dash and questionable if there were any such capital. Beware of them. Insolvent Dec 1841*
9[2]	*The father of the Paisley Water Company bringing water to Paisley his sole hobby for 70 years*
10[3]	*14 years in trade – coarse buckrams – are in good credit and stay cautiously though not wealthy*
12	*A young man son of 16 below depending on his father for means who may have lent him a little*
13	*Insolvent 2 or 3 years ago Poor*
16[4]	*Father of 12 [James] wealthy. Has some good well-paying property and a first rate trade*
17	*Respectable a good business and easy in circumstances*
20[5], 21	*An old established house in easy circumstances Some good property and an excellent trade. Old man retired, trade carried on by the 2 sons (21) one of the sons carrying on a separate trade besides the thread in the same work*
26[6]	*Both father & son dead. Grandson and nephew carries on the trade. Wealthy and an excellent business. Have good property*
28	*Supposed the wealthiest manufacturer in Paisley Has escaped all the disaster of this year 1841. Has extensive property Gas, Water &c shares*
29	*Very wealthy retired called Property Kerr to distinguish him*
32[7]	*Brother of 20 & 21 [John] partner in the concern*

PAISLEY. 51

Kerr, William, surgeon—house 7 Orr square
2— Kerr, William, upholsterer, 43 High street
Kessan, John, grocer and spirit dealer, Lylesland
Kessan, Mrs, dressmaker, 11 Wardrop street
Keter, Thomas, grocer, 17 Inkle street
6 —Kibble, James, of Whiteford, residence Greenlaw house,
7 Kibble, Mrs. James, of Greenlaw, Greenlaw house
8 —Killoch, John, spirit dealer, 10 Williamsburgh
Kilpatrick, Hugh, tailor, 40 Causeyside
Kilpatrick, Hugh, tailor, 103 High street
Kilpatrick, Thomas, tailor, 40 Storie street
King, Agnes, enterer, 12 Barr street
13 —King, Alexander, merchant, (Coffee Room Buildings, Cross,) 107 High street—ho. 16 Moss street
King, Alex., of Russell & King—ho. 4 Clark's place
King, Hugh, clothier, 2 St. Mirren street
King, James, spirit dealer, 37 St. James' street
King, John, *late trumpeter of the 16th Light Dragoons*, 9 Canal street
King, M., enterer, 48 Storie street
King, Mrs., feuar, 3 New Smithhills
King, Mrs., flesher, 11 Smithhills
King, Mrs., linen dresser, 9 Canal street
King, Mrs. William, Lonend
23 —King, Walter & John, contractors and builders, orders left at King, Alex., merchant, 107 High st. (Cross)—residence Houston
King, William, enterer, 13 Buchanan street
King, William, weavers' wright, 58 Broomlands
Kinninmont, Isabella, grocer & spirit dealer, 5 Williamsburgh
27 —Kirkland, John, manufacturer, 13 Canal street—ho. 11 Barclay street
Kirkland, Mrs T., dressmaker, 65 Love street
29 —Kirkland, Robert, clothlapper, 112 Causeyside—house 5 Orchard street
30 — Kirkwood, Allan, writer, 3 Moss street—ho. Netherfield.
Kirkwood, Thomas, grocer and spirit dealer, 19 Maxwellton street
Kirkwood, Wm., grocer & cowfeeder, 3 Maxwellton st.

Entry	**Page 51**
2	*Very poor. Paid 1/- composition in 1829 and has never since got into credit*
6	*Bankrupt printer[1] broken down and living with his mother, No.7 [Mrs James Kibble], whom he secured in a good mansion before he failed*
8	*Has considerable means, bank stock &c., and is daily improving it*
13	*Has been 19 years in the same shop never has acquired a good share of the trade, is cautious and counted safe. Is a brother of Walter below*
23	*Successful undertaking. Are industrious. Have 2 or 3 thousand spare money always in their Bank account. Have had large contracts on the Railway*
27	*Very easy in circumstances. Does a triffling business. Has his money lent out*
29[2]	*Worth about £1,000. Has in ordinary terms the best trade of the line in the town*
30	*Beware of him. Has been guilty of signing other people's names than his own without a per pro. The Western had two bills which his father paid*

Knox, James, clock and watchmaker, 80 High street—
house 8 Orr square
Knox, John, spirit dealer, 100 George street
Knox, J. and R., joiners and timber merchants, 20 New Sneddon
Knox, Robert, clock and watchmaker, 64 High street

LAIRD, Jas., iron founder, 89 New Sneddon—ho. 37 do.
Laird, John, perfumer, and hair cutter, 10 St. Mirren st.
Laird, Mrs. John, dressmaker and milliner, 92 High st.
Laird, Robt., of Mackie & Laird—house 3 Back Sneddon
Laird & Thomson, shawl manufacturers, 3 Cumberland court, 110 Causeyside
Lamb, James, architect and surveyor, Underwood street, and iron merchant, 4 St. James' place
Lamb, Robert, clerk at John Hart's, writer, 87 High street—ho. 21 Niddry street
Lambie, Andrew, hairdresser, 37 Moss street
Lambie, Mrs., Burns' place
Lang, Alexander, manufacturer, 59 George street
Lang, Gavin, of Lang & Wilson—house 22 Moss street
Lang, James, boot and shoemaker, 70 Broomlands—house 11 King street
Lang, James, East Relief church officer and house factor, 10 Thread street
Lang, James, treasurer and manager Canal Company, 18 Canal street—house 10 Barclay street
Lang, John, dyer and renovator, and general washing field, Espedair street
Lang, John, grocer and spirit dealer, 9 West Campbell st.
Lang, Malcolm, late dyer, Burns' place
Lang, Mrs , feuar, 8 Smithhills
Lang, Peter, causeyer and cowfeeder, 33 Moss street
Lang, R. W., manufacturer, 7 St. Mirren street
Lang, Robert H., foreman at M'Arthur, Robert, & Co. dye-works, 8 Marshall's lane
Lang, Robert, manufacturer, 17 Wardrop street
Lang & Wilson, writers and town clerks, County Buildings
Langmuir, James, victualler, 75 Broomlands
Langmuir, Mrs., grocer, 8 Lawn street

Entry	**Page 52**
2[1]	*Of no means. His brother made money in the shop, but ruined himself and was turned out by law expences incurred contesting a seat at the Police Board*
3[2]	*1833 began without means. 1836 in good credit 1839 the largest dash in town 1841 sequestrated*
4	*An eccentric odd character. A wit*
5[3]	*Son newly succeeded to his father. His father Bankrupt many times totally without means, but good trade not taken care of. Beware*
9[4]	*Insolvent of no worth*
10	*A good business in iron and coal and respectable as an architect and surveyor*
14[5]	*Not wealthy but quite safe. Not of the speculation caste*
16	*Has been for the past 20 years reputed to be easy in circumstances*
19	*Dissipated low character*
21[6]	*Retired wealthy*
23	*Above the common run of cowfeeder. Has small means.*
24	*Partner of 7, page 50, Kerr & Co*
26	*Insolvent*
27	*Respectable. Lang [is] wealthy*

Langmuir, Robert, flesher, 20 Causeyside—house do.
Langmuir, William, grain merchant and miller, 19 Thread street—house 1 Cart street.
Latin, Samuel, hairdresser, 45 George street
Latta, John, cowfeeder, Canal side, Millerston
Latta, William, plasterer, 8 Abbey street
Lauder, Alexander, smith, copper and tin-plate worker, 1 Water brae, New Smithhills—house 28 do.
Lawrie, Wm., jun., confectioner, 15 Smithhills—ho. do.
Lawson, John, currier, 17 High street
Lawson, John, Hamilton Farm coal yard, 11 New street—house 6 Stow street
Lawson, Mary, grocer, 20 St. James' street
Lawson, William, ironmonger, 109 High street
Leckie, Arch., of Wark, Leckie, & Co.—ho. Blackhall
Lee & Love, dressmakers, 12 George street
Lee, James, farmer, Stanley
Lee, Mrs., corset and dress maker, 5 Hospital lane
Leggat, David, gardener and cowfeeder, 36 Lady lane
Leggat, James, gardener, 38 Lady lane
Leighton, Robert, builder, 44 Moss street
Leiper, Alexander, feuar, Gateside
Leishman, John, grain merchant, 8 Orr square,—house 47 Oakshaw street
Leitch, John, joiner, cabinet maker, and lappet wheel cutter, 7 East Buchanan street (opposite Catholic Chapel)—Furniture warehouse, do.
Leitch, Peter, porter, 9 New street
Leitch, William, tailor, 25 High street
Leitch, William, warper, 12 Prussia street
Light, John, flower lasher, 10 Orchard street
Lindsay, Walter, smith and farrier, 80 Canal street
Litster, Mrs., grocer, 5 Castle street
Livingston, Alexander, nailmaker, 34 Thread street
Livingston, Malcolm, cowfeeder, 17 George street
Lochhead, Alexander, spirit dealer, Three mile house
Lochhead, James, coal merchant, 14 Abercorn street
Lochhead, John, draper, 100 High street—house 86 do.
Lochhead, John, farmer, Ingleston
Lochhead, Math. of Kerr, Peter, & Son—ho. 28 George st.

Entry	**Page 53**
1	*In good credit and respectable trade*
2[1]	*Was once very wealthy. Lost a large sum by guaranteeing Canal bills which were fixed on him and others by Court of Session. Lost £2,000 by Miller his son in law in 1830. Much pitied. Has a considerable quantity of good house property, mill &c <u>and no bonds December 1841</u> but sometimes scarce of money for his business*
6	*Insolvent brought down by Holms and Andrew*
7	*Easy in means. Is proprietor of the house he occupies. Has a good business. House free*
11	*Almost a miser. Has an excellent trade, but much cut down in profit by so many upstarts <u>now</u> to contend with supposed worth two or three thousand pounds*
18	*Miserably poor*
19[2]	*Very wealthy and retired*
20	*Insolvent offering 6/-*
21	*Very poor, not in credit property bonded*
26	*Disreputable no means*
30	*Insolvent every 2 or 3 years*
33[3]	*Son of John Lochhead late grocer in town who died last year leaving £10,000. Six of a family. Well doing and industrious, easy in means*

Lochhead, Mrs., (Railway Tavern,) 7 Renfrew street
Lochhead, Robert, manufacturer and grocer, 36 Canal st.
Lochhead, William, grocer, 2 Causeyside—house do.
Lochrie, Manasses, grocer, 2 Lawn street
Lockhart, J., turner and wheel wright, 38 Wellmeadow
Lockhart, William, feuar, Espedair street
Lodge, Benjamin, tailor, 18 Sandholes
Lodge, John, manager at Carriagehill factory
Logan, David, spirit dealer, 2 Garthland street
Logan, James, of West March
Logan, Thomas, grocer, 118 George street
Lorimer, John, 8 West Croft street
Lorimer & Douglas, smiths and farriers, 1 Burn row
Lorn, James, baker, 5 George street
Loudon, James, wholesale grocer, 35 Wellmeadow
Loudon, William, tailor, 5 George street
Love, Angus, cloth merchant, 12 George street
Love, James, keeper of the Paisley Coffee Room—house 12 School wynd
Love, Mrs., teacher and straw hat maker, 4 Neilston st.
Lowe, William, bookbinder, 2 New street
Lowndes, Charles, manufacturer, 80 New Sneddon
Lowndes, Wm. and Jas. & Co. manufs., 80 New Sneddon
Lowndes, William, of Arthurlie—house 79 New Sneddon
Lupin, Mrs., druggist, 5 Storie street
Lyall, George, wine and spirit merchant, 94 New Sneddon—ho. 25 Moss street
Lyall, James, of Lyall, Wm. & Sons—ho. 90 High st.
Lyall, Wm., of Lyall, Wm. & Sons.—ho. 18 Oakshaw st.
Lyall, Wm. & Sons, wholesale grocers and drysalters, 40 New street, and grocers, 90 High street
Lyle, Jas., clothlapper, 23 Causeyside—ho. 4 Wardrop st.
Lyle, Wm., toy, basket, and brush shop, 91 High street
Lymburn, Jas., clerk Saucel Brewery Co.—ho. 10 Saucel
Lymburn, Jas., of Lymburn, Jn., & Sons—ho. Burns' place
Lymburn, John, and Sons, silk mercers, leghorn and straw hat manufacturers, 15 High street
Lyon, Andrew, agent Ayr railway, Gilmour street—house 3 Garthland lane
Lyon, James, hosier and grocer, 19 Barclay street
Lyon, James, joiner and cartwright, 4 Inkle street

Entry	**Page 54**
2	*Has some property and means in trade does a small business. Quite safe*
3[1]	*Brother of 32 [John], prior page. Old son and retains the family business of which he was partner the first twelve years (John Lochhead & Son). Wealthy*
5[2]	*Has some good property clear and money but in ackers – good going business and easy in means*
6[3]	*Had much property bonded to more than its present depressed value., Is in abject poverty*
10[4]	*Very wealthy. Retired paper maker*
14[5]	*An excellent business and easy in means has £500 lent on Bakers mill in town*
15[6]	*Insolvent offering 5/- per pound*
17	*Failed in 1828 and has never got on since was ruined in trade and means by engaging extensively in Cloth Clubs*
21, 22[7], 23	*[Charles and William of Wm and Jas. & Co. Lowndes] Supposed wealthy and the supposition surely well founded. An expensive aristocratical family, and conducts their business on an old expensive system. William, one of the partners of the late Paisley Bank. Charles not a partner – very dissipated and allowed to job about the warehouse*
25	*Worth December 1834 £3,000, lost part of it in 1836 but cannot be much poorer (of any) excellent business and well managed*
28	*Had to execute a statement of his affairs in consequence of being deeply involved with his son in law (J Gentles). Showed assets £13,000 engagements £7,000, December 1841*
30	*Easy in circumstances has always money in bank*
33	*Old established wealthy house said to be leaving the town in consequence of property being so cut down by upstarts*

MACK, Andrew, hatter, 28 High street—ho. Blackhall
Mack, John, jun., spirit dealer, 1 Burn row
Mack, John, sen., spirit dealer, 1 Saucel bridge, Bladda
Mackay, George, superintendent Renfrewshire rural police —house 4 Bank street
Mackie, George, teller Bank of Scotland—house 17 Causeyside
Mackie and Laird, linen and woollen drapers, 33 High st.
Macome, Alex., of Macome and Hartley—house Daisy bank, 24 Back Sneddon
Macome and Hartley, town's commercial and mathematical school, 4 Meeting house lane
Mair, Jn., boot and shoemaker, 3 High st.—ho. 32 Glen st.
Mair, John, & Co., joiners and cartwrights, Lonend
Mair, John, & Son, leather merchants, 3 High street
Maitland and Alexander, cabinet makers and weavers' wrights, 2 West brae—furniture warehouse, 15 Wellmeadow
Maitland, James, spirit dealer, 24 George street
Malcom, David, spirit dealer, 10 Orchard street
Malcom, Mrs., grocer, 56 Causeyside
Malcom, William, cowfeeder, 5 Bridge street (burgh)
Manson, James, draper, 89 High street
Manson, Jn., clerk at Baird & Wallace—ho. 58 Storie st.
Manson, Misses, milliners and dressmakers, 38 New street
Manson and Son, reedmakers, 39 New street—ho. 38 do.
March, Thomas, schoolmaster and session clerk, 31 Storie street—house do.
Mardock, Wm., boot and shoemaker, 28 Lady lane
Marshall, Hugh, spirit dealer, 78 Canal street
Marshall, John, manufacturer, 4 Cumberland Court, 110 Causeyside—house 13 Stevenson street
Marshall, J. R., teacher of music and piano forte, &c., precentor U.S.C., (No. 3)—house 5 St. James street
Marshall, Miss, milliner, 34 Moss street
Marshall, Samuel, boot and shoemaker, 18 New Sneddon
Marshall, William, accountant, 4 Moss street—house 1 Water brae (burgh)
Marshall, William, baker, 6 Broomlands
Martin, Alexander, cutler and gun maker, 71 High st.— house 28 Oakshaw street

Entry	**Page 55**
1	*Has apparently a fair business, and judging from his Bank operations, does not seem to be distressed for means at anytime*
2	*Son of John sen. No means*
3[1]	*Had apparently an excellent business but to the surprise of everyone declared insolvent this year*
6	*Set up by the late William Symington, on the eve of failing, M & L being two of his shopmen. Had no means. Have astonished everyone how they have got on. Have opened a dashy shop in Greenock this year. Beware*
9	*Old established shoe shop never supposed to have great means. Great puffer*
10	*Insolvent. Property bonded*
11	*Same as No.9 – John Mair, sole partner*
17[2]	*Insolvent rouped out*
20[3]	*Very poor. In consequence of accommodation with H Thomson they mean time suspended payment*
24	*Quite unknown some set up of a commission house*
28	*Will have money by his wife. Is always engaged in disreputable affairs*
29	*Poor poor – In no credit – In debt*
30[4]	*Long established. Has some property and is considered safe*

Martin, James, smith, 5 Bridge street (Newtown)
Martin, John, carding master, Adelphi mill, 68 New Sneddon
Martin, John, grocer, 9 Seedhill
Martin, Matthew, baker, 13 Smithhills
Martin, Michael, fruit and egg dealer, 11 Cotton street
Martin, R. and J., ship owners, 7 West Croft street
Martin, Thomas, contractor, 12 Dyer's wynd
Martin, William, writer, 1 Smithhills—house Beauchamp place, 42 Love street
Mason, Arch., of Mason, Arch. & Son—house 3 Great Hamilton street
Mason, Archibald & Son, manufacturers, 18 Causeyside
Mason, A. and T., coal merchants, 7 Abercorn street
Mason, Gavin, grocer, 28 Thread street
Mason, Miss, furnished lodgings, 73 Causeyside
Mason, Thos., of Mason A. and T.,—ho. 7 Silk street
Mason, Thos., of Mason, Arch. and Son—house 1 Garthland street
Masson, George, of Masson, George and Son—house 2 New Smithhills
Masson, George and Son, thibet croppers and shawl cutters, Cumberland factory, Laigh Kirk lane
Masson and Harris, blacksmiths, iron plough makers, and farriers, 5 Back Sneddon street
Masson, Mrs. George, stay and bandage maker (successor to Mrs. Broadwood) 61 High street
Masson, Mrs. William, corset and dressmaker, 60 High street
Masson, Peter, thibet cropper, shawl and cheneille cutter, Cumberland factory, Laigh Kirk lane—house 27 Back Sneddon
Masson, Thomas, shoemaker, 2 Wellmeadow
Mathieson, John, tailor, 18 Abbey close
Mavitie, Charles, of Hodge and Mavitie—ho. Blackhall
Maxwell, Alexander, tailor, 3 Lawn street
Maxwell, James, of Brediland and Merksworth—residence Merksworth Cottage
Maxwell, Mrs., general grocer, 15 Old Sneddon
Maxwell, Misses, milliners and dressmakers, 94 Causeyside

Entry	**Page 56**
6[1]	*Wealthy. Has much excellent property in town and several vessels all clear. Lately manufacturers. Western Bank shareholders – Are misers*
8[2]	*Respectable old established business of Martin, Simpson & Martin – has means*
10	*Insolvent – Disreputable*
11	*No means and very limited credit – beware of them*
17	*Well-spoken of. Made a little money in the Lisbon trade. Has a son there considered safe*
21	*Poor foolish dissipated creature. Son of 17 [George] without means or credit*
24	*Dead October 1841*
26	*House of old standing but now on its last legs. Poor & dissipated estate under Trust*
27[3]	*Husband absconded to America in 1833 creditors took all. A well doing woman but without means. A good run and making day & way*

Maxwell, William, grocer and spirit dealer, 16 Gauze st.
Maxwell, Wm., shawl manufacturer, 115 Causeyside
Meikle, Archibald, (No. 3) U. S. C. officer, 8 Love st.
Meikle, R. C., clerk Saucel brewery Co.—ho. 1 Christie st.
Meikleham, John, teacher, (Hutcheson's school) Orr st.
—house 8 Orr square
Meiklewee, William, grocer, 25 New Smithhills
Meins, Mrs., grocer, 12 New Sneddon
Mellis, William, agent, 17 Broomlands
Mellis, W. & J., painters and paper hangers, 99 High st.
—workshop 14 do.
Mellis, William, victualler, 17 Broomlands
Mellon, John, hairdresser, 32 Moss street
Melville, John, flower lasher, 162 George street
Melvin, Miss A., straw hat maker, 38 Ferguslie
Melvin, Thomas, weavers' furnishing shop, 17 Broomlands
Melvin, Wm., jun., & Co. cloth merchants, 97 High st.
Menzies, Archibald, hosier, 117 George street
Menzies, Graham, distiller, King st. Saucel—ho. do.
Menzies, Robert, sen.—house 15 Maxwellton
Menzies, Robert, spirit cellars, 75 Broomlands—do. 2 Saucel
Merrylees, John, manufacturer, 169 George street—house View bank
Merrylees, Miss, milliner and straw hat maker, 16 Cotton st.
Merrylees, Robert, clerk, Paisley Commercial Bank—house View bank
Middleton, David, spirit dealer, 12 West Croft street
Middleton, James, brewer, Lexwell brewery, Millerston
Millar, Adam, manufacturer, 15 Prussia street—house 2 Christie street
Millar, Adam, tinsmith, 9 St. Mirren street
Millar, Alex., gardener, 19 Well street
Millar, Andrew, writer, 4 Smithhills—ho. 40 Oakshaw st.
Millar, Arthur, spirit dealer, 77 Broomlands
Millar, David, & Son, tailors, 103 High street
Millar, George, cowfeeder, 73 Canal street
Millar, George, excise officer—house 28 Wellmeadow
Millar, George, foreman printer, at M'Kechnie, Kerr, & Co.—house 43 New street

Entry	**Page 57**
2	*Insolvent. Composition 4/6*
9[1]	*Poor. Not long in business*
14	*Without means*
15[2]	*Successor to Arch Stewart – his old shopman – succeeded to a good business – without means – careful and industrious – leader of the Volunteers*
20[3]	*Has considerable means. Proprietor of Calside house and grounds. Does but little business Not speculative*
23	*Dissipated foolish character*
24	*Failed in 1839 – still poor*
25	*Insolvent. Composition [blank]*
26	*Poor*
28	*Good business Means upwards of £1,000 known*
30[4]	*Has some valuable property and a good business*

Millar, George, manufacturer, 8 Causeyside—house 24 Ferguslie
Miller, James, manager, Blackhall factory—ho. Lonend
Millar, James, silk mercer, 9 High street
Millar, John, of Barr & Millar—house 103 High street
Millar, John, carter and coal dealer, 2 New Sneddon
Miller, John, carter, 93 New Sneddon
Millar, John, copper and tinsmith, 82 High street
Miller, John, manufacturer, 4 Orchard street
Miller, John, teacher, 59 Storie street
Millar, Mrs. John, milliner and dressmaker, 92 High st.
Millar, Thomas, spirit dealer, 31 George street
Millar, Walter, superintendent for Abbey parish poor, 9 Gauze street—house 29 New Smithhills
Miller, Wm., jun , middle church officer, 2 Maxwell st.
Miller, William, sen., town drummer, bill distributor and poster, 20 School wynd
Miller, William, weavers' office, 150 George street
Miller, Robert, yarn bleacher, 4 Clark's place, Seedhill— house 3 Christie street
Milligan, Edward, cowfeeder, 33 Wells street
Milliken, Mrs., broker, 19 Wellmeadow
Mills, Charles, foreman at Coats, J. & P.—house 14 Ferguslie
Mills, James, pattern drawer, 3 Wardrop st.
Mills, Peter, builder, 92 Causeyside
Mitchell, Andrew, plasterer, 149 George st.—ho. 150 do.
Mitchell, Arch., turner and vintner, 27 Wellmeadow
Mitchell, Daniel, pawnbroker, 31 High street
Mitchell, James, broker, 13 New Smithhills
Mitchell, James, dyer, 17 Abbey close
Mitchell, Jas., governor of prison—ho. County Buildings
Mitchell, John, boot and shoemaker, 4 Broomlands
Mitchell, John, farmer, Patterhill
Mitchell, John, teller, Paisley Commercial Bank—house 4 Smithhills
Mitchell, John, dealer in teas, fruit, &c., teacher of deaf and dumb, 43 High street
Mitchell & King, coal agents, storers of heavy goods, and weighers of carts, 16 Old Sneddon

Entry	**Page 58**
1[1]	*Insolvent. Composition [blank]*
2[2]	*The remains of the once great John Millar & Sons who introduced the rich shawl trade to Paisley*
3[3]	*Was Millar & Smith last year Smith appointed surveyor of taxes. Steady. Industrious and though of limited means in good credit and good business secured*
7	*Father of 26 [Adam] prior page – Poor*
8	*Only 6 months in trade. Son of 2 [James] above. Has no means. Cannot get on but as a jobber to Harvey Brand & Co his father's employers in the Factory*
9	*A poor dissipated teacher with property bonded beyond value*
16	*Poor Poor. Can never pay his way. Bills often laying over*
21[4]	*Poor*
23	*Very poor Failed in 1831*
24[5]	*Has by industry acquired means. Has an excellent business many years in the spirit line*
26	*Insolvent. Had money but brought down by the desperate times*
28	*A tolerable poet. Has several small works published, but poor as a church mouse.[a] Should stick to his last*
29	*Has means. Married 1837 widow Lochhead who has a good annuity from her late husband's property*

---

[a] For example, *A Wee Steeple's Ghaist and Other Poems and Songs*, published by Murray & Stewart, Paisley 1840

Mitchell, Thomas, spirit dealer, 85 Causeyside
Mitchell, William, pattern-drawer, at M'Arthur, Robert, & Co.—ho. 28 St. James' street
Mitchell, William, teacher, 10 Gauze st.—ho. 3 Lawn st.
Moffat, John, builder, 33 Thread street
Moir, Mrs., milliner and straw hat maker, 23 George st.
Molloy, Duncan, shoemaker, 4 Silk street
Money, John, teacher, Paisley educational association school, Carbrook street
Monoch, James, manager at M'Kechnie, Kerr, & Co.—ho. 11 New street
Montgomery, Wm., cashier and surveyor of Police assessment, County Buildings—ho. 9 Cross street
Morgan, John, of M'Kerrell & Morgan—ho. Camphill
Morgan, Robert, grocer and spirit dealer, 62 High st.
Morren, George, German clock maker, 47 High st.
Morris, Andrew, flower lasher, 2 Wardrop st.
Morrison, Alex., & Co., clothlappers, 15 Causeyside
Morrison, Alexander, grocer, 7, Old Sneddon
Morrison, George, spirit dealer, Lylesland
Morison, James, manufacturer, and jacquard machine maker, 16 Causeyside—ho. 2 Thread street
Morrison, James, wine and spirit merchant, 45 Broomlands, and brewer, Braehead brewery
Morrison, Mrs., leghorn and straw hat maker, 14 Wardrop street
Morton, Henderson, shoemaker, 34 Glen street
Morton, James, boot and shoemaker, 139 George street
Morton, John, leather cutter, boot and shoemaker, 9 Smithhills—ho. do.—boot and shoe shop, 100 High st.
Morton, John, of Morton, John & Co.—house 38 Causeyside
Morton, John, & Co., shawl manufs., 38 Causeyside
Morton, Mrs., grocer, 4 Abbey close
Morton, Thomas, shoemaker, 16 Back row, Sandholes
Morton, W. L., flower lasher, 1 Stevenson street
Motherwell, John, nailmaker, 7 Orchard street
Motherwell, N. C. G., druggist, 17 High street
Moyes, Geo., starcher, George place—ho. 83 High st.
Muir, Andrew, feuar, 16 Wellmeadow

Entry	**Page 59**
1	*Poor Was all last month in jail for debt, involved in cautionry & suffered for it*
10	*Has small means. Has a very limited business*
15	*Poor Has often to be assisted by his brother James below in his distress*
16	*Sequestrated. Composition offered 1/4*
17	*Has been long in business and has, in ordinary times a good one. In good credit <u>and said</u> to be doing well*
23	*Had once (7 years ago) considerable means. 3 years ago all gone. Highly respected honourable house, but must be poor. Beware of them. Are in tolerable credit withal*
29[1]	*Has no means. Failed in 1826 and in 1830. A soft honest man and cannot get on in the world*

Muir, Archibald, teacher, 7 Seedhill
Muir, Catherine, earthenware dealer, 4 Causeyside
Muir, Hugh, grocer and ham-curer, 24 Wellmeadow
Muir, Hugh, spirit dealer, 11 Moss street
Muir, James, grocer & spirit dealer, 23 Stock street and 13 Neilston road—house 1 Smith street
Muir, James, slater, 13 Broomlands
Muir, John, accountant, and agent for Globe Insurance Co., 22 Moss street—house 52 Love street
Muir, John, shawl manufacturer, 4 Cumberland Court, 110 Causeyside—house 140 George street
Muir, John, victualler, 25 Gauze street—house do.
Muir, John, writer, 31 Gauze street
Muir, John, yarn merchant and warpor, 109 Causeyside
Muir, Joseph, & Co. pawnbrokers, 3 Neilston street
Muir, Matthew, grain dealer—house Greenhill
Muir, Robert, baker and grain merchant, 46 Moss street
Muir, Robert, carter, 26 Queen street
Muir, Robert, jun., feuar, 13 Stevenson street
Muir, Robert, sen., feuar, 1 Stevenson street
Muir, W., grain dealer and miller, Saucel mills—house 7 Burn row
Muir, Wm., grocer and grain merchant, 93 High street—house 20 do.
Muir, William, pawnbroker, 39 Gordon's lane
Muirhead, Andrew, boot and shoe maker, 20 Glen street
Mullen, Hugh, tailor, 47 Hamilton street, Charleston
Mungle, Hugh, baker, 4 Smithhills
Mungle, Hugh, spirit cellar, 10 Well street
Mungle, John, teacher, 3 Mile house, Glasgow road
Munn, A. & M., shawl merchants, 112 Causeyside
Munn, Armstrong, manufacturer, 35 Storie street
Munn, D., surgeon, oculist, and druggist, 31 Causeyside
Munn, James, manufacturer, 18 Causeyside—house 13 George street
Munn, Matthew, of Munn, A. & M.—ho. 6 Garthland st.
Munn, Mrs., spirit dealer, 12 Abercorn street
Munn, William, carter, 22 Orchard street
Munro, James, tailor, 4 Broomlands
Munro, John, tailor, 44 Moss street

Entry	**Page 60**
2	*A small dealer, but has money in Western Bank these some years*
5	*Well-spoken of. Said to have considerable means. Has in ordinary times a good business. In a bad corner of the town in such times. Surrounded by weavers*
8	*Father died 1832 leaving considerable means. A cautious trader. Considered safe. Has considerable house property but his mother liferented*
10[1]	*Much money in the family left by an uncle. Has liferent by courtesy. Is poor, but a respected old man. Dean of Faculty for past 20 years*
11[2]	*A triffling trade. Small means*
13[3]	*Not in business. Merely salesman to his brother No.18 [William] below*
14	*Very wealthy. Excellent trade. Shares in most of the public companies. Had in 1830 £1,800 lent on property Broomielaw and sums elsewhere*
16, 17[4]	*Heirs of the late David Walker. Has both some good property*
18[5]	*Excellent business. Respectable. Said to have considerable means*
19	*Easy in circumstances. Good business and safe*
20	*Has some means. Is in but a small way*
23	*Constantly in difficulties. Poor poor*
25	*Insolvent. Composition [blank]*
26[6]	*Father of 25 [26, A & M] wealthy. Has heavy sums lent out on bond. Cautious and but a small trade in the manufacturing line*
27	*Drunken old fool of police notoriety*
28	*Failed in 1826. Again in 1841 and now (Dec) down on composition*

Munroe, David, tailor, 89 High street
Murdoch, James, boot & shoe maker, 6 Sir Michael street
Murdoch, John, book agent for Blackie & Sons, Glasgow
—house 2 Wardrop street
Murdoch, John, wine & spirit mercht., 29 New Smithhills
Murdoch, P. & Son, clothiers and hatters, Gilmour street
Murdoch, P., of Murdoch, P. & Son—house Gilmour st.
Mure, Jas., porter Bank of Scotland—ho. 117 Causeyside
Murehead, James, baker, 18 Lady lane
Murphy, Thomas, pattern drawer, 109 High street
Murray, David, painter, paper-hanger, oil and colourman, Gilmour street—house do.
Murray, George, and Co., manufacturers, 112 Causeyside
Murray, James, furnished lodgings, 3 Back Sneddon
Murray, John, carter, 10 Back row, Sandholes
Murray, John, shawl manufacturer, 115 Causeyside
Murray, Jos., of Murray & Stewart—house 8 Orr square
Murray, Matthew, carter, 31 Cotton street
Murray, Matthew, spirit dealer, 2 Garthland street
Murray, Miss Marion, grocer and earthenware dealer, 6 St. Mirren street
Murray, Mrs., straw hat maker, 41 High street
Murray & Stewart, booksellers, stationers, and bookbinders, 6 High street
Murray, William R., pattern drawer, 50 High street
Murtrie, W., surveyor and collector for the Water Company—house 7 Oakshaw street

MACALISTER, Alexander—house 17 Storie street
Macalister, Andrew—house 25 Calside
Macalister, John—house Blackland place
Macalister, Mrs., grocer, 24 New Smithhills
Macalister, William, jun.—house Blackland place
Macalister, William, sen.—house 25 Calside
Macalister, Wm. & Sons, manufacturers, 15 Causeyside
M'Alpine, John, coal merchant, 4 Middle lane
M'Alpine, William, tailor, 9 High street
M'Arthur, Henry J., shawl manufacturer, 3 Forbes' place—house 54 High street
M'Arthur, James, feuar, late manufacturer—ho. Camphill

F

Entry	**Page 61**
5	*Too many irons in the fire. In Gilmour street shoe shop. Known to be poor and has got assistance lately from friends*
10[1]	*Has property in Gilmour street worth £500 debt £160. Got other property left him last year. Good business but being chief magistrate is over the ears in municipal affairs. Has his name on community's bills which being insolvent will ruin him*
11	*Have not <u>gone out</u> in the late speculation. Have some means, and are taking care of them. Left last year a little house property by their father. Careful company*
14	*Insolvent as Semple and Murray*
20	*Respectable trade, but in these times not paying them. Are separating. One of them goes to Glasgow <u>it is said</u>*
23[2], **24**[3], **26**, **27**[4], **28**[5]	*[Andrew, John, William, jun., William, sen., of Macalister, Wm & Sons] A very wealthy family of rather a mean caste. Old man made much money in the Hamburgh trade end of last century and family have improved it ever since. Property, shares, money lent &c &c. Do but a small trade*
32	*Insolvent. Composition 16/- was worth £3,000 in January last. Was brought down in a <u>scandalous</u> manner by Dick making a large purchase 20 days before he failed*
33[6]	*Father of the above, wealthy*

M'Arthur, John, clothier, 16 Moss street
M'Arthur, John, grocer and spirit dealer, 21 Wallace st.
M'Arthur, Miss, milliner & straw hat maker, 93 High st.
M'Arthur, Mrs., milliner & dressmaker, 48 Moss street
M'Arthur, Robert, & Co., shawl manufacturers, 7 and 8 Forbes' place
M'Arthur, Robert, of M'Arthur, Robert, and Co—house 6 East Buchanan street
M'Arthur, Wm., manufacturer, 15 Causeyside—house 16 do.
M'Ausland, Robert, boot and shoe maker, 14 High street —house do.
M'Beath, John, tailor, 7 Abbey street
M'Bride, Hector, cowfeeder, 24 Love street
M'Bride, John, farmer, Kelburne Cottage
M'Bride, Neil, farmer, West March
M'Call, James, chimney sweep, 8 New Smithhills
M'Callum, Alex., grocer & spirit dealer, 7 Love street
M'Callum, Alex., grocer and spirit dealer, 4 Neilston road
M'Callum, Archd., skinner, 6 New Smithhills—house 8 Lawn street
M'Callum, John, cowfeeder, Ferguslie Walk
M'Callum, John, teller, Glasgow Union Bank, 109 High street—house, 3 New Sneddon
M'Callum, Neil, foreman at Carlile, James, and Son, 13 Carlile place
M'Call, Mrs., green shop, register office for servants, 21 Moss street
M'Cargow, Adam—house 5 West brae
M'Clymont, Mrs., grocer, 18 Storie street
M'Connal, William & Co., brokers, 78 High street
M'Conochie, Bannatyne, baker, 12 High street
M'Conochie, James, shuttlemaker, 134 George street
M'Corry, P., Edinburgh clothes' shop, 5 St. Mirren st.
M'Coull, George, foreman, Bladda dyeworks, 6 Bladda—house 12 Saucel
M'Credie, Samuel, tailor, 29 High st.
M'Crossan, Mrs., tailor and clothier, 2 Storie street
M'Crone, John, manufacturer, 7 Back row, Sandholes
M'Culloch, John, Blackhall and Causeyside toll bars

Entry	**Page 62**
2	*Has some means. A good business and shares in Paisley Commercial. In an excellent part of the town among public works*
5	*Was in 1837 worth £15,000 lost 4 or 5,000 after that year. Made up considerably next two years. Invested too much in property and partially embarrassed themselves. Have still considerable means. An excellent maker but does too much*
7[1]	*Brother of the above [Robert, 5 and 6]. Has a large amount of good paying property. Does almost no business. Is very dissipated – or rather takes 3 or 4 days hard drinking once a month. Sometimes deranged with it. Is wealthy*
8[2]	*Is wealthy. Much by his father in the wholesale leather trade. Son improving what was left*
21	*Wealthy. Retired living on rents*
30	*Failed last year paid nothing*

M'Dermid, Mrs.—house 1 Orr square
M'Devat, Mrs., clothier, 16 St. Mirren street
M'Donald, Alex., spirit dealer, 5 East Buchanan street
M'Donald, Alex., jun., spirit dealer, 3 Lillias' wynd
M'Donald, Alex , wine and spirit merchant, 11 Canal st. —house 9 do.
M'Donald, D. & J. & Co , manufacturers, 104 Causeyside—house 49 Love street
M'Donald, Daniel, spirit merchant, 16 Lawn street
M'Donald, Hugh, feuar, 13 Millerston
M'Donald, James, cowfeeder, 8 Smithhills
M'Donald, John, corkcutter, 42 Moss street
M'Donald, John, keeper Abbey Sounding Aisle, 9 Abbey close—house 6 Abbey street
M'Donald, Mrs. John, tailor, 9 High street
M'Donald, Mrs., straw hat maker, 6 Silk street
M'Donald. Neil, late manufacturer—house 49 Love st.
M'Donald, Robert, boot and shoe maker, 2 Gauze street
M'Donald, Thomas, sexton, Abbey burying ground—house 7 Smithhills
M'Dougal, Alex., cowfeeder and spirit dealer, 5 Silk st.
M'Dougal, John, brewer, 1 Ferguslie, East lane
M'Dougal, John, broker, 29 Causeyside
M'Dougal, Lieut. Colin, 27 Millerston
M'Dowall, Andrew, agent Glasgow Railway, Gilmour st. —house 73 Love street
M'Elmail, Peter, surgeon, 91 High street
M'Ewen, Alexander and Co., hatters, 102 High street
M'Ewen, Mrs., linen dresser, 2 Gauze street
M'Fadyen, Findlay, (New Town Inn) 9 Gauze street—coaches, chaises, hearses, gigs, &c.
M'Fadyen, James, grocer and grain dealer, 33 High st., and 86 Causeyside
M'Fadyen, John, beamer, 15 Castle street
M'Fadyen, Mrs. Archd., cowfeeder, 5 Cotton street
M'Fadyen, William, stocking maker, 18 Sandholes
M'Farlane, Alex., postmaster, Gilmour street—house 15 High street
M'Farlane, Alex., teller British Linen Company Bank —house 2 Caledonia street

Entry	**Page 63**
6[1]	*Has only an agency in town. Gone to Glasgow*
8[2]	*Easy in the world retired manufacturer*
12	*Poor lost her all by fire 1833*
14	*Wealthy has large sums lent out and much valuable property*
18[3]	*Industrious but without means. Knows his business well was "Cheaps", afterwards "Buchanans" famed salesman.[a] Commenced in 1834*
22[4]	*Has considerable means. Western Bank shares &c*
25	*Failed in 1837 brought down by James MacFarlane & Co. Well doing industrious man. In tolerable credit again. Was imposed on by JMcF*
30	*Discharged for embezzlement, cautioner paid £500 to government*

---

[a] James Chep (*sic*) ("Cheaps" above) was a partner in James Chep & Co., who held the Sacell Brewery from 1810 to c.1831, when his share sold to other partners. A later partner in the Sacell Brewery was Edward B. Buchanan, who died in 1839. (See Gibb and Close, p. 63, also Borland's Fowler page 79, p. 135 of this volume, no. 11)

M'Farlane, Daniel, of Canal Bank.
M'Farlane, Ebenezer, C. (No 4) U. S. C. officer, 24 George street
Macfarlane, Hugh and Son, manufacturers, 3 Cumberland Court, 110 Causeyside—house 56 Love street
M'Farlane, James, feuar, Chapel House, Blackhall
M'Farlane, James, Glenpatrick
M'Farlane, John, Stanely Castle tavern, 9 Prussia street
M'Farlane, Jos., grocer and cowfeeder, 21 New Smithhills
M'Farlane, Kenneth, grocer and spirit dealer, 20 Seedhill
M'Farlane, Misses, dressmakers, 27 New Smithhills
M'Farlane, Mrs. A., spirit dealer, 1 Garthland street
M'Farlane, Mrs., waste and rag store, 83 Broomlands
M'Farlane, Mrs. Robert, 2 Caledonia street
M'Farlane, Robert, tailor, 3 South Croft street
M'Farlane, T. H., wine and spirit merchant, 29 Lady lane—house Canal Bank
M'Farlane, Walter, collector of poors' rates (for burgh,) 30 St. James' street
M'Farlane, Walter, of M'Farlane, W. and W.—house George place
M'Farlane, W. and W., timber merchants, joiners, and *Steam Saw Mills*, George place
M'Farlane, Walter, pastry baker and spirit dealer, 66 Broomlands
M'Farlane, Wm., bookbinder and paper ruler, 46 High street, and 4 New street
M'Farlane, William, hairdresser, 4 New street
M'Farlane, Wm., of M'Farlane W. & W.—ho. George pl.
M'Fee, Alexander, flower lasher, 8 Forbes' place
M'Fee, Daniel, boot and shoe maker, 73 Broomlands
M'Fee, Duncan, smith, 73 Broomlands
M'Gallan, David, tailor, 14 St. Mirren street
M'Gavin, David, tailor, 45 High street
M'Gavin, Miss—house 31 Glen street
M'Gaw, Joseph & Son, tailors and clothiers, 12 St. Mirren street, and 24 Wellmeadow
M'Gechan, James, manufacturer, 16 Causeyside
M'Gee, John, grocer, 13 Abbey street
M'Gibbon, John, wright and timber mercht., 52 High st.

Entry	**Page 64**
1[1]	*Retired distiller wealthy*
3[2]	*Had 18 months ago £8,000. Undertook along with a partner Cessnock Iron Works, Ayrshire. Differed with partner who March last advertised out. Has laid out £11,000 on works. Works not paying. Manufacturing concern suffering with the times. Insolvent. Composition to company creditors and to private creditors*
4	*Has a large quantity of low property*
5	*Failed 1830 paid 5/- 1837 paid 3/- living on wife's annuity – dejected*
13[3]	*Has a good business and in good credit, considerable demurring and doubling when his brother No.5 failed. In both cases quite clear, said now to be easy. Son of No.1 [Daniel]*
16	*Are industrious easy traders, means unknown but seem to be easy. Five years in town. Have a fair business*
21, 22	*[Daniel and Duncan] Of little note save for the noise they make at election times. Beware*
28	*Insolvent. Composition [blank]*
30[4]	*A decayed old man. Insolvent 1825 business wholly by son, 2 [Walter] next page*

M'Gibbon, Misses, dressmakers, 10 Abbey street
M'Gibbon, Walter, ironmonger, 51 High street
M'Gill, James, boot and shoe maker, 52 George street
M'Gill, William, boot and shoe maker, 39 New street
M'Gilvray, Alexander, baker, 25 Causeyside
M'Gilvray, John, baker, 152 George street
M'Gillivray, Duncan, feuar, Blackhall
M'Goun, Andrew, agent and coal merchant, Harbour lane—house 12 New Sneddon
M'Gown, James, beamer, 17 Back Sneddon
M'Gown, John, wine and spirit merchant, 96 Causeyside, and grocer and spirit dealer, 18 Seedhill
M'Gown, Mrs. George, linen dresser and furnished lodgings, 1 Lilias' wynd
Macgregor, Duncan, of Greive, Macgregor & Co.—house 26 Orchard street
M'Gregor, Gregor, clerk, at Wark, Leckie, & Co.'s—house 22 Caledonia street
M'Gregor, John & Co., calico, silk, and woollen printers, Patrick Bank—counting house, 76 Virginia street, Glasgow
M'Gregor, John, foreman, baking association, 21 New Smithhills
M'Gregor, John, of M'Gregor, John, & Co.—house Patrick Bank
M'Gregor, Thomas, hairdresser, 31 Moss street
M'Guire, John, porter, 16 Causeyside
M'Guire, Thomas, joiner and cartwright, Stanely
M'Haffie, James, power loom factory, 15 Abbey close
M'Houl, Andrew, spirit dealer, 9 Orchard street
M'Hutcheon, Mrs. Jn., grocer & spirit dealer, 20 Cotton st.
M'Hutchison, James, musician, 6 Abbey street
M'Hutchison, Mrs., milliner, 12 High street
M'Ilwham, William, beamer, 38 Stock street, Charleston
M'Ilwrick, Thomas, warper, Cart lane
M'Indoe, John, cowfeeder, spirit and potato dealer, 3 King street
M'Indoe, Robert, furnishing shop, 7 Gauze street
M'Innes, John, spirit dealer, 20 Abbey street

Entry	**Page 65**
2	*Principal business a joiner. Has means, about £2,000. Is industrious and a good business. The best of the time in town. In good credit. The ironmongering shop kept by his father, John preceding page, but wholly the son's*
5[1]	*Has made a little money. Has a good business, and doing well*
7[2]	*A tricky low character. Fails every 2nd or 3rd year. Insolvent 1841. Shun him*
8	*Dead. Widow carries on coal trade. Poor*
10	*Insolvent*
14	*Sequestrated 1841*
18	*Has made a little money, an industrious tradesman. Bought last year his paternal cabin in the vicinity of Cork out of love for the spot*
20	*An agency from Glasgow*

M'Intosh, James, manager at Buchanan, Walter & Co.'s, Blackland mill
M'Intosh, William, dyer, 6 Snodgrass lane, Seedhill—house 13 Bath place
M'Intyre, Duncan, spirit merchant, 44 New st.—ho. 3 do.
M'Kaig, James, mason, 19 Moss street
M'Kaig, Miss, dressmaker, 9 Back Sneddon
M'Kaig, Mrs, register office for servants, 11 Moss street
M'Kay, Alex., collector of road money for Abbey parish, 53 High street
M'Kay, Archd., boot and shoe maker, 6 Wellmeadow
M'Kay, Jean, green grocer, 49 Moss street
M'Kean, James, late clothier, 28 Glen street
M'Kean, Robert, of Sim, William & Co.—house 29 New Smithhills
M'Kechnie, Alex, manufacturer, 21 Glen street
M'Kechnie, Daniel, grocer and spirit dealer, 46 New Sneddon
M'Kechnie, John, grocer, 29 Causeyside
M'Kechnie, Kerr & Co., manufacturers—silk, worsted, calico, and shawl printers, Cumberland place, Laigh Kirk lane—sale warehouse, North court, 22 Exchange square, Glasgow
M'Kechnie, Peter, shoemaker, 5 Lawn street
M'Kechnie, Robert, jun., of M'Kechnie, Kerr & Co.—house 10 Smithhills
M'Kechnie, Robt. and Wm, M D., 10 Smithhills—ho do.
M'Kellar, Donald, carter and cowfeeder, 2 Silk street
M'Kell, John, hairdresser and perfumer, 4 Moss street
M'Kenzie, Daniel, clerk of prison—ho. County Buildings
M'Kenzie, Daniel, gardener, Renfrew street—shop 6 Smithhills
M'Kenzie, Hugh, boot and shoe maker, 44 Causeyside
M'Kenzie, Hugh, of M'Arthur, Robert & Co.—house Renfrew street
M'Kenzie, John, road and well contractor, 3 Broomlands
M'Kenzie, John, engineer and board smith, Adelphi mill, 68 New Sneddon
M'Kenzie, Miss, dressmaker, 74 Love street
M'Kenzie, Mrs., broker, 27 Moss street

Entry	**Page 66**
2	*Had much money. Not yet insolvent but has suffered dreadfully this year. Beware of him. Failed in 1829*
3	*Was almost ruined 1837 by J McFarlane but paid his way. Is undoubtedly poor*
12[1]	*Has had nothing but the name for 5 years. No means. No credit*
13	*Poor poor. Property bonded*
14	*Well doing careful man. In good credit and a good business but very limited means*
15	*Sons of very wealthy parents. Has means of their own though limited for the trade they do. Has several thousand pounds from their friends particularly McKechnie. Have a good business and seemingly doing well. Are industrious and careful*
17	*Father (Robert) of the above. Has considerable sums lent, and much good house property. An excellent business of the better classes*
19[2]	*Dissipated creature*
21	*Left 3 years ago. Considerable means, mother an old woman life rented in the property, and by a blunder in the will moveables cannot be touched till her death £1,700 in Bank then*
23	*A brother [of 21]*
24	*Poor*

M'Kenzie, Neil, grocer and spirit dealer, 15 Williamsburgh
M'Kenzie, Rev. Thomas, A.M.—house 7 Hunter street
M'Kerrell, James, weaver's office, 25 Lawn street
—M'Kerrell and Morgan, manufacturers, 110 Causeyside
M'Kerrell, Miss, Brabloch
M'Kerrell, Mrs. Jn., grocer and spirit dealer, 25 Lawn st.
M'Kerrell, William, of M'Kerrell and Morgan—house 3 Garthland place
—M'Kinlay, Daniel, M.D., 42 New street
—M'Kinlay, James, Water Company's civil engineer—ho. 1 Maxwellton
M'Kinlay, John, spirit dealer (carriers' quarters) 35 High street
M'Kinlay, Robert, cowfeeder, 21 School wynd
M'Laggan, Alex., broker, 81 Broomlands
M'Lachlan, David, grocer and victualler, 97 Causeyside
M'Lachlan, Dugald, boot and shoe maker, 11 Gauze st.
M'Lachlan, Duncan, gardener and cowfeeder, 17 Well st.
M'Lachlan, Mrs., milliner & straw hat maker, 47 Moss st.
M'Lachlan, John, cowfeeder, 3 Bladda
M'Lachlan, Miss Janet, dressmaker, 13 Gauze street
—M'Lachlan, Rev. Robert—house 56 Canal street
M'Lardy, Alex., copper and tin plate worker, 30 Gauze st.
M'Laren, James, teacher of Abbey parish school, 8 Thread street—house do.
M'Lean, Andrew, dyer, 8 Dyer's wynd—ho. 59 Love st.
M'Lean, James, gardener, 28 Cotton street
—M'Lean, John, dyer, 8 Dyer's wynd—house Gateside, Inchinnan
M'Lean, John, teacher, 75 Causeyside
M'Lean, Miss, dressmaker, 92 Causeyside
M'Lean, Mrs., eating house, 14 Moss street
M'Lean, Mrs., grocer, 9 School wynd
M'Lean, Mrs. John, weavers' office, 94 Causeyside
—M'Lellan, John, muslin manufacturer, 4 Gauze street—house 26 Causeyside
M'Lellan, Misses, milliners and dressmakers, 69 High st.
M'Lellan, William, beamer, 12 Neilston road
M'Lerie, David, pattern drawer, 9 Gordon's lane

Entry	**Page 67**
4[1]	*Wealthy. Grant no bills. Are highly respectable. Have a good business*
6	*Common brothell of long standing*
8[2]	*Has an excellent practice of a second rate class of the inhabitants*
9	*A well informed man. On his practical knowledge that the fame of the "Thoms" as to waterworks depend, he was long their servant[a]*
19[3]	*Independent preacher confines himself entirely to his duties. No politician*
24	*Failed in 1837 and the surprise is that he is not down this year. Has had terrible losses. Has a good country trade which may have saved him at this time*
30	*Newly commenced with about £500 of capital. Is doing little yet. Was Brough and Sharps pattern drawer*

---

[a] Loch Thom, in the Clyde Muirshiel Regional Park above Greenock, supplies 5 6 miles of aqueduct bringing water to the town to power the mills. It was designed by Robert Thom (1774-1847) and opened in 1827

M'Lerie, Joseph, pattern drawer, 9 Gordon's lane
—M'Lerie, Mrs. David, grocer, earthen and stoneware dealer, 29 New street
—M'Lerie, M. and J., furnishing shop, 102 Causeyside
—M'Lerie, Mrs. Patrick, grocer, 39 Ferguslie
M'Lerie, Thomas, warper, 89 Causeyside
M'Lerie, Miss, milliner, 94 Causeyside
—Maclurkin, Thomas, pawnbroker, 98 Causeyside, and 1 Queen street
M'Manus, John, rag and waste store, 42 Lady lane
M'Menamy, Edward, broker, 77 High street
M'Millan & Brown, spirit dealers, 20 Old Sneddon
—M'Millan, Duncan, spirit dealer, (from Earl Grey Inn,) 43 Moss street
M'Millan, John, twiner, 27 New Sneddon
M'Millan, Miss, milliner and dressmaker, 27 New Sneddon
M'Millan, Neil, warper, 26 Causeyside
M'Murchy, John, clerk, Blackhall factory
M'Nab, Andrew, of Barr & M'Nab—ho. 8 Abercorn st.
M'Nab, Malcolm, bookseller, 5 Broomlands
—Macnair, Rev. Robert, Abbey Manse
M'Nair, Archibald, of M'Nair & Brand—house 5 Garthland place
—M'Nair & Brand, silk and shawl merchants, 1 Causeyside
—M'Nair, David, general grocer and victualler, 97 Causeyside, 3 Smithhills, and 37 High street—house 6 Brown's lane
M'Nair, James, broker, 21 Moss street
M'Nair, Jas., manuf., 4 Forbes' place—ho. 6 Stow place
M'Nair, Robert, farmer Meikleriggs
M'Nair, Walter, spirit dealer, 12 Saucel
—M'Nair, William, grocer and spirit dealer, 72 Causeyside
—N'Naught, John, broker, 37 New street
M'Naught, John, reporter for the Paisley Advertiser newspaper—house 38 Storie street
M'Naught, Miss J., dressmaker, 8 Back Sneddon
M'Naught, Mrs. Neil, oil and colour shop, 1 St. Mirren st.
M'Naughtan, Colin, clothlapper, 28 New street—house 6 Orchard street

Entry	**Page 68**
2[1]	*Husband vanished in 1824. Has brought up her family respectably since he left her. Is industrious and has a little credit*
3	*Concern belongs to the mother who has money as widow Weir*
4[2]	*Left a widow 1836 with considerable means and house property. Is improving what was left*
7	*A good deal of money in the family Mrs Blair the mother in law a partner with considerable means*
11	*A silly body. Failed many times both as a manufacturer and spirit dealer. In no credit Has no means*
18[3]	*Attends to his duty unlike his colleague and many others of the profession who are all politicians*
20	*Very wealthy. Brand gave £8,000 for Barshaw House and grounds this year. Excellent business*
21	*Good business and easy in his circumstances. Doing well*
(23)	*Dead*
26	*Brother of 21 [David] but limited in means. Not the tact of his brother*
27	*Very poor, behind with his rent*
29	*A poor widow struggling for a livelihood*

—M'Naughtan, James. shawl manufacturer, 113 Causeyside—house 1 Oakshaw head
—Macnaughtan, Rev. John, A.M.—house Castlehead
—M'Neil, James, clothier, Gilmour street—house do.
N'Neil, John, broker 82 Broomlands
M'Neilledge, Misses, dressmakers and milliners, 101 High street
M'Nicol, Alexander, grocer, 148 George street
—M'Nicol, Archibald, shawl manufacturer, 2 Silk street
M'Nicol, Duncan, farmer and grazier, Inch cottage
M'Nicol, Mrs., eating house, 7 New street
M'Nicol, William, at M'Arthur, Robert, & Co's. jacquard weaving factory, 14 Causeyside—ho. 25 Glen st.
M'Nish, William, boot and shoe maker, 51 Storie st.
M'Oscar, William, classical teacher, 87 High street
—M'Phee, Duncan, sheriff-clerk's office, County Buildings—house 22 Causeyside
M'Pherson, Alexander, sizeing master, Adelphi mill, 68 New Sneddon
M'Pherson, Alexander, tailor, 8 New Smithhills
M'Pherson, Archibald, manager, Adelphi mill, 68 New Sneddon—house do.
M'Pherson, Dugald, spirit dealer, 29 New Sneddon
M'Pherson, James, Bailie of Abbey Burying Ground—house 2 Gauze street
M'Pherson, John, tailor, 148 George street
—M'Pherson, William, writer, 5 Christie Terrace—house 16 Moss street
—M'Queen, Alex., cabinet and chair warehouse, 9 Wellmeadow st.—ho. do.—workshop, 3 Barclay st.
M'Queen, John, manager, Thread Work, 8 St. James' st.
M'Rae, Alexander, broker, 69 High street
M'Rae, Arthur, spirit dealer, 21 Broomlands
M'Taggart, Lachlan, tailor, 24 New Smithhills
M'Taggart, Mrs., cowfeeder, 48 High street
M'Vay, John, porter, 107 Causeyside
M'Viear, Peter, grocer, spirit and coal dealer, 6 Union st.
M'Walter, Mrs., milliner and corset maker, shawl border and fringe shop, 45 Causeyside
M'Walter, Mrs , spirit dealer and eating house, 46 High st.

Entry	**Page 69**
1	*Insolvent. Composition 3/-*
2[1]	*Leader of the Non-Intrusionists. A popular preacher*
3	*Insolvent*
7	*A new name without means or trade*
13	*The only sober Sheriff Officer in the town*
20[2]	*Disreputable. Married last year a Miss [Mrs?] Thomson who had money in her own right.[a] Got it on pretence of lending it. Spent the money £300 and gave her fictitious bonds to deceive her*
21	*[Blank]*
28[3]	*Has considerable means and some good house property*

---

[a] Margaret Thomson's marriage took place on 27 October 1838 (ScotlandsPeople), but marital status is unstated. She was 20 at time of marriage and had a daughter aged two according to the 1841 census. Thee is no further census record of the husband.

1 —NAIRN, Andrew, accountant & house factor, 3 Moss st.
—house 13 Thread street
Nairne, William, treasurer Gas Company, 22 Moss street
—house 3 Caledonia street
National Security Savings' Bank, 4 Christie Terrace
4 —Napier, John, collector of prison and rogue money, 4
Moss street—residence Blackstoun
5 —Napier, Matthew, cabinet maker & joiner, 58 Causeyside
—house 52 do.
Neil, Miss Frances, grocer 10 Gauze street
Neilson, Geo., clerk at Whyte, James, jun.,—ho. 6 Love st.
Neilson, James, carpet shoemaker, 11 John street
9 —Neilson, John, printer, paper ruler, bookbinder and stationer, 15 St Mirren st.—ho. 21 St. James' street
Neilson, Matthew, baker, 24 High street
Neilson, Matthew, heddle maker and weavers' office, 40 George street
Neilson, Mrs., feuar, 1 Silk street
13 —Neilson, Thos., joiner & cabinet maker, 6 Wellmeadow
Neilson, Thomas, traveller, 8 Abbey street
Neilson, William, spirit dealer, 29 Orchard street
Neilson, William, teacher, 52 George street
Neilson, William, teacher, 16 Thread street
Nichols, James, grocer & spirit dealer, Blackhall
Nicol, Alex., boot and shoe maker, 22 Broomlands
Nicol, George, beamer, 25 West street
Nicol, Miss, straw hat maker, 22 Broomlands
Nicol, Robert, salesman to Holms, Alex., victualler—
house 6 Wardrop street
23 —Nicol, Walter, manufacturer, 115 Causeyside—house 31 Glen street
24 Nisbet, Rev. William, U. S. C.—house 48 Oakshaw street
Niven, John, salt dealer, 38 Broomlands
Niven, Miss M., tuscan and straw hat maker, 100 George st.
Niven, Robert, carter, 4 Old Sneddon
Norrie, John, at Reid, John & Co's nursery, Linside
79 —Notman, Mrs. William, cowfeeder, 87 Causeyside.

OAKES, Alexander, broker, 79 High street
O'Donnell, Mrs., broker, 31 New Smithhills

Entry	**Page 70**
1	*Thirty years the manager of the late firm of Wm Fulton & Sons. Attempted manufacturing since but could not get on Tried a grocery which did not succeed. Trying factorage for a livelihood. Poor*
4	*Poor. Brother of Napier of Blackstoun who got him the place*
5	*Poor. Once much property in the family now all gone*
9	*A good going business but a foolish manager. The writer saw his balance sheet last week (20 December 1841). Capital in trade £220. Has besides the half of the Paisley Advertiser Newspaper which has, for the last ten years, given him £80 annually, can be sold for £500 – that price is offered*
13[1]	*Of old standing. Has, in ordinary times, a good trade*
23[2]	*Insolvent. Has signed trust deed composition apparently 7/-*
24[3]	*Popular leader at public meetings. A poor preacher*
29[4]	*Life rented in some respectable good tenanted property. No bonds*

O'Hara, Daniel, broker, 79 High street
O'Hara, Peter, tailor, 58 Back Sneddon
Oliver, Archibald, grocer, 34 Glen street
Oliver, John, teacher 8 Barr street
Oliver, Robert, tobacconist, 83 Broomlands
O'Neil, Henry, broker, 2 Lawn street
O'Neil, Patrick, spirit and provision dealer, 20 Moss st.
Orchison, George, tea dealer, 24 Maxwellton
Orr, Andrew, ale, wine, and spirit merchant, 12 High st.
Orr, Charles, writing master, 16 High street
Orr, James, grocer, 1 East Croft street
Orr, John, jun., & Co. cotton spinners, Underwood street
Orr, Misses, 22 St. James' street
Orr, Mrs. William, sen.— house 54 Love street
Orr, Robert, of Orr, Wm. & Robert—ho. 54 Love street
Orr, Robert, builder, 24 Storie st.—stone yard 9 George st.
Orr, Robert, stocking maker, 41 New street
Orr, Wm. & Rt., manufacturers, 106 Causeyside—James Dykes, agent—counting house 39 West Nile street, Glasgow
Osborne, James, weavers' wright and turner, 20 Lawn st.
Ostler, Andrew, miller, Bakers' mill, Camphill
Oswald, James, tea merchant, 160 George street

PAISLEY Advertiser Office, 15 St. Mirren street, published on Saturday morning at 7 o'clock
Paisley Coffee Room and News Room, 107 High street, (Cross) James Love, keeper—house 12 School wynd
Paisley Directory Office, 57 Canal street, G. Fowler
Paisley Library, 4 Moss street, John Muir, librarian
Paisley and Renfrewshire Reformer Office, 19 High street, published on Saturday at 5 evening
Park, Alex., general grocer, 106 High street (Cross) and 97 Causeyside—house 45 New street
Park, Allan, Gockston
Park, John, jun., late manufacturer—house Gockston
Park, Mrs. James, manufacturer, 12 Gauze street
Park, Mrs., milliner, 27 High street —
Parker, Misses, dressmakers, 89 High street
Parker, Wm., flower lasher, 13 Wardrop street

Entry	**Page 71**
5	*Long in trade but is not supposed to have made much money*
7[1]	*Deacon in Catholic Church. Has an excellent trade with the Irish by whom he is much looked up to. A clever intelligent man much respected by all parties*
8	*Careful and industrious Gave £180 this year for the house he lives in which was (in the Western) all saved by economy and industry*
9	*Has a respectable house, good business, and is reported to have made some money. Long in the line*
12[2]	*Dead. Has left considerable means. The son carries on the spinning business but gives up other branches in which his father was partner. See W Philips &c*
16[3]	*Not wealthy, but has some means and a little property. In ordinary times a good town trade*
(17)	*Poor*
18	*A new agency on Paisley. Must have taken considerable means from the town when they left it*
19	*Leader of the Chartists – A fool*
22	*Circulation 600 Editor's salary £120 Printing £6 – 10 a week. Profit £160 a year for the last ten years – halfed between Rob Hay editor and John Neilson printer – Tory paper*
26	*A Glasgow paper with papers sent to Paisley and assumes the name – Liberal paper*
27	*Insolvent 1840. Doing no good. The public accuses him of some low tricks as excise informations &c against people he had trepanned. The Bank knows him as guilty of higher crimes. Beware*
28, 29[4]	*[Alan and John] Wealthy. In no business. Retired*
30[5]	*A strange character morally speaking but has considerable means. Does but little as <u>a regular</u> manufacturer*
(31)[6]	*Respectable*

Parkhill, John, newspaper reporter, 12 John street
2 —Paterson, Alex., grocer and grain mercht., 62 Causeyside
Paterson, Hugh, tailor, 8 Christie street
Paterson, John, pattern drawer, 9 Orr square
Paterson, Matthew, cowfeeder, 34 Canal street
Paterson, Mrs., nail manufacturer, 11 Orchard street
Paterson, Peter, farmer, West March
Paterson, Robert, spirit dealer, 117 George street
9 —Paterson, Wm., flesher, 2 Smithhills—house 19 do.
Paterson, William, grocer, 54 Canal street
11 —Paton, Alex., Scotch & English cloth merchant, 89 High st.
12 —Paton, James, M.D., 33 Old Sneddon—consulting rooms, 48 Moss street
Paton, John, boot and shoemaker, 88 Canal street
Paton, John, cowfeeder, 40 Gordon's lane
15 —Paton, John, woollen and linen draper, 103 and 104 High street, (Cross)—house 45 Oakshaw street
16 —Paton, John, grocer, 34 High street
17 —Paton, Mrs., linen & woollen draper, 102 High street
Paton, Mrs. James, flesher, 3 Abbey close
19 —Paton, Robt., joiner, cabinet maker, and timber mercht., 4 St. James' place—furniture warehouse do.—ho. 11 do.
20 —Paton, Thomas, coal agent, 89 Canal street
21 —Patrick, James, manufacturer, 7 St. Mirren street
Patrick's fashionable boot and shoe warehouse, 86 and 87 High street
Patrick, Robert, London hat warehouse, 87 High street—house 86 do.
Pattison, James, farmer, Holland Bush
Pattison, Robert, blacksmith, 9 Gauze street
26 —Pattison, Robert, merchant, 42 High street
Pattison, Thomas, bill-poster and deliverer, 93 High st.
Pattison, William, land surveyor, 42 High street
Paul, John, cowfeeder, 26 New street
Peacock, Andrew, clerk, power loom factory 15 Abbey close—house 21 Cotton street
Peacock, James, keeper Hillington toll bar
Peacock, John, auctioneer and appraiser, auction mart, 83 High street—house 7 Gauze street
33 —Peacock, William, baker, 73 Causeyside

Entry	**Page 72**
2[1]	*Insolvent 1840. Having the name of some means he involved all his neighbours in twenty or thirty pounds each – poor poor, but ought to have done well*
9[2]	*Insolvent 1836 or 7 Has married a managing woman since. Has a tolerable share of the trade. Still poor*
11	*One of the annuals which continually infect the trade of Paisley. Has no means. December 1841 Bills laying over*
12[3]	*Purchased the business of the late Dr White a few months before his death for £800. A dislocated thigh got at the time prevented him from following up the advantage. The money was lost. Is now 1841 very poor and little employ*
15[4]	*Remains of the old business of the late Alex Paton. Has had an excellent trade for the last 15 years. In good credit and considerable means*
16[5]	*Nicknamed "Split the Pea" for his narrowness. Has made some money. Is almost out of trade, and will not risk it again*
17[6]	*Mrs Climie, but transacts her business in the name of her last husband, older brother of 15 [John] (See Climie). Has a good business and easy*
19[7]	*An unfathomable character. Fond to be thought wealthy. A private discounter and has suffered to a great extent this year. Always in confusion. One of the Magistrates – beware*
20	*Some property which will give no rents this year. Counted easy in circumstances*
21[8]	*Only 6 months in trade no means, not yet failed*
26	*In no business. Very wealthy – see James Stirrat page 85*
33[9]	*Has a good business and comfortable. Has good property, cost 1,500 all clear and rents well – quite safe*

Pearson, James, lath splitter, 66 Love street
Pearson, John, supervisor, office 109 High street—house 28 New Smithhills
Peden, J., accountant, British Linen Company's Bank—house Gallowhill Cottage, Renfrew road
Penfold, George, agent Greenock railway, Gilmour st.—house Underwood street
Peock, Mrs., of Meikleriggs
Perrie, Thomas, spirit dealer, 18 Moss street
Perrie, Wm., sen., hair dresser and umbrella maker, 65 George street
Perrie, William, toll keeper, Moss toll bar
Petrie, James, house factor, 72 Broomlands
Philips, George, grocer, 64 Millerston
Philips, John, boot and shoe maker, 5 St. Mirren street
—Philips, Peter, joiner and cabinet maker, 32 Gauze street—furniture warehouse 31 do.
—Philips, Wm., agent for the London Royal Exchange Assurance, 6 Forbes' place—ho. 2 Caledonia street
—Philips, Wm., & Co., silk & yarn merchts., 6 Forbes' place
Phillips, Capt. Robert, barrack master, barracks, Williamsburgh
—Pinkerton, Alex., feuar—house 1 Garthland street
Pinkerton, James, printer, Trades' Temperance Coffee House, 24 High st.
Pinkerton, John, cabinet maker, 39 Wellmeadow—furniture warehouse, do.
—Pinkerton, John, surgeon, 36 High street—ho. 1 Garthland street
Pinkerton, L., tinsmith and gas fitter, 43 Moss street—work shop, 42 do.
—Pinkerton, Mrs. Alex., feuar, 1 Garthland street
Polin, Edward, stationer and news agent, 16 Causeyside
Pollock, Alexander—house 10 Barclay street
—Pollock, Alexander, cotton yarn merchant, 8 Causeyside—house 5 Neilston street
Pollock, James, grocer and spirit dealer, 23 New Sneddon
—Pollock, James, silk and yarn merchant, 21 Causeyside—house Greenhill
Pollock, Mrs. Peter, 10 Barclay street

Entry	**Page 73**
(12)	*Poor*
13[1], 14	*William & William & Co., Company dissolved. The business now carried on by WP solely. Is in good credit and some means. The company lost considerably this & last year but divided a large amount. The new concern has not lost much*
16[2], 19[3], 21	*(16, 19, 21) Mother and two sons with great abundance. Immense good house property, and all daily making more*
(20)	*Poor*
24	*Not wealthy. His father failed in 1828. Is careful industrious and in good credit. Has lost much this year – beware!*
26[4]	*Has ranked this year for £9,000. Is supposed to have more than £10,000 left. Takes no credit Barclay & Pollock in 1824 Barclay's widow took out £10,000*

Pollock, Mrs., stay and corset maker, 4 Storie street
2 —Pollock, Nathan, grocer, 26 Broomlands
Pollock, Robert, baker, 6 Silk street
Pollock, William, spirit dealer, Carriagehill
5 —Polson, John, buckram and shawl manufacturer, 2 Cumberland Court, 110 Causeyside—house Thurscraig
Polson, William—house Orr street, Lylesland
Poole, Alexander, artist, 70 Love street
8 Porteous, Dundas, engineer and machine maker, 1 Calside —house 43 do.
9 —Porter, J. & J., manufacturers, 105 Causeyside
Porter, James, of Porter, J. & J.—house 129 George st.
11 —Porter, James, merchant, 23 Glen street
Porter, John, of Porter, J. & J.—house 7 Wardrop st.
Post Office, Gilmour street, Alex. M'Farlane, postmaster
Pratt, Alex., cabinet maker and funeral undertaker, iron mortsafes supplied, 34 Gauze street—ho. 5 Abbey st.
15 —Provan, W. & H., manufacturers, 114 Causeyside
Provan, William, of Provan, W. & H.—ho. 4 Bank st.
Pullar, Charles, boot and shoe maker, 68 Causeyside
Purcell, Rev. James, Catholic clergyman—house 2 East Buchanan street
Purdon, James, slademan, Sacell Brewery Co., 9 Saucel
Purdon, John, cowfeeder, 12 Abercorn street
Purdon, Mrs. A., milliner and straw hat maker, 59 High st.

QUIGLEY, James, teacher, Catholic school, 5 Orr st.— ho. East Buchanan street
Quigley, John, tailor, 6 Smithhills

RALSTON, Archibald, wright, 54 George street
Ralston, John, grocer, 54 George street
Ralston, John, grocer, 9 New Sneddon
27 —Ralston, Wm. & Co., merchants, 109 Causeyside—ho. 31 High street
28 —Ramsay, Mrs., flesher, 1 George street
29 —Rankin, John, brick builder, 71 Love street
Rattray, Miss Isabella, dressmaker, 9 Orr square
Rattray, Miss Jane, straw hat maker, 9 Orr square
Rayside, James, feuar, 142 George street

Entry	**Page 74**
2	*Had to retire in 1838 from a respectable thread concern from dissipation. Has that vice kept in check by his wife. Has some good property saved from the old concern. Old work which belongs to the family 5 years shut up*
5	*Individual partner of Brown & Polson. Does too much business for means. Highly dangerous to be trusted individually*
8[1]	*Poor poor*
9[2]	*Insolvent. Composition 6/6*
11[3]	*Has about £5,000 in his business £10,000 in the 4 percents in which his father, aged 84, is life rented. His father had £24,000 left him 10 years ago. Has two sons, the subject of this and John in America not heard of these several years. The writer of this executor on the wills of the parties*
15[4]	*Insolvent, will have no composition*
27	*Insolvent, composition 7/-*
28[5]	*A poor widow brought to misery by ill-doing father & son. Husband stabbed himself in his bedroom and died instantly. Son out of the way*
29	*Has had, for ten years, the best trade in the line in the town. Industrious and attentive and acquiring means*

Rea, John, dyer, 12 Niddry street—house 11 do.
Reformed Synod's Divinity Hall, 38 Oakshaw st., Rev. Andrew Symington, D.D., Professor
Reid, Archd., mashman, Saucel Distillery, King street, Saucel—ho. 12 do.
Reid, David, spirit dealer, Three Mile Cottage
Reid, Francis, spirit dealer, 1 Bridge street, Newtown
Reid, Hugh, clerk at T. H. Macfarlane's, 29 Lady lane——ho. 41 George street
Reid and Hanna, smiths and iron boat builders, 12 High street, main entry by Laigh Kirk lane, Causeyside
Reid and Henderson, writers, Gilmour street
Reid, J. & J., dyers, 12 New Smithhills
Reid, James, farmer, Meikleriggs
Reid, James & Co., manufacturers, 5 Causeyside
Reid, James, musician, Salutation Inn, (carriers' quarters) 29 High street
Reid, John, clerk, Bank of Scotland—ho. 108 George st.
Reid, John, joiner, cartwright, and timber merchant, Lylesland—house do.
Reid, John & Co., nursery and seedsmen, 3 Moss street, nursery Linside, Seedhill
Reid, John, session clerk for Middle Church parish, and teacher of Town's English school, 19 School wynd, —house 25 Moss street
Reid, John, simple tyer, 57 Canal street
Reid, John, wigmaker and haircutter, 98 Causeyside
Reid, Miss E., milliner and straw hat maker, 15 George street
Reid, Mrs., dressmaker, 22 Causeyside
Reid, Mrs. John, druggist, 108 George street
Reid, Mrs. John, fruiterer and seed shop, 35 High street
Reid, Mrs., milliner and dressmaker, 8 Well street
Reid, Robert, feuar, 19 Wellmeadow
Reid, Robert, grocer, 20 Abbey street
Reid, Robert, grocer, 5 Moncrieff street
Reid, Thomas, painter, 93 High street—house 94 do.
Reid, William, of Reid & Hanna—ho. 34 High street
Reid, William, of Reid & Henderson—house Linside
Relief Synod's Divinity Hall, 32 Thread street

Entry	**Page 75**
1[1]	*Insolvent for the third time. A well doing man, but has always had an abominable set of customers*
5	*Made about £1,000 in the spirit line 6 years ago bought a farm which has ruined him Has again commenced his old line meantime – poor*
7[2]	*Considerable means. Good work clear and a most excellent business*
8[3]	*Extensive practice. Reid considerable means and a good conveyancer. Henderson a good court man*
9[4]	*Scarcely has got an existence*
10	*Father in Kilbarchan parish and has means. Son easy in circumstances*
11	*Insolvent offers 9/-*
14	*Insolvent second time*
15	*Left considerable means by his father. Has a good business. Brother of 7 [Reid and Hanna]*
24[5]	*Made considerable means as a grocer and grain merchant, of long standing, retired wealthy*

1 —Renfrew, John, smith and farrier, 1 Williamsburgh
Renfrew, Mrs., milliner, 8 Moss street
Renfrewshire Directory Office, 57 Canal street
Renfrewshire Reformer Office, (Paisley and) 19 High st.
    published on Saturday at 5 evening
Rennie, George, flesher, 17 George street
Rennie, James, flesher, 28 George street, and 148 do.
Rew, James, tailor, 24 Cotton street
Rice, Samuel, victualler, 46 Broomlands, and 69 do.
Richardson, John, High Church officer, 86 High street
Richardson, Mrs. John, Burns' place
Richmond, Daniel, of Richmond, Thomas, & Son—house
    82 High street
12 —Richmond, Mrs., biscuit baker, 4 St. Mirren street
Richmond, Thomas, of Richmond, Thomas & Son—ho.
    82 High street
14 —Richmond, Thomas, & Son, surgeons, 82 High street
Rigg, John, clerk British Linen Company's Bank—ho. 73
    Causeyside
16 —Risk, Thomas, manager Paisley Commercial Bank, 4
    Smithhills—house Burns' place
17 —Ritchie, David, wholesale general grocer and tea merchant, 8 Gauze street
18 —Ritchie, James, & Co., wrights and timber merchants,
    Three Mile House, Glasgow road
Ritchie, Mrs. William, grocer, 20 School wynd
Ritchie, Wm., Friendly Society clerk, 17 Barclay street
Robb, Richard, cowfeeder, 16 Inkle street
22 —Robb, Wm. and Co., manufacturers, 6 Causeyside
Robertson, Alex., of Wilson & Robertson—ho. 8 George st.
Robertson, Andrew, enterer, 32 George street
Robertson, Andrew, spirit dealer, 5 Well st.—house 4 do.
Robertson's basket and toy shop, 8 Moss street
27 —Robertson, Daniel, gardener, 3 Smithhills
Robertson, Daniel, sexton, 14 Oakshaw street
Robertson, David, flower drawer, 27 Orchard street
30 —Robertson, J. & J., shawl manufacturers, 24 Causeyside
Robertson, James, church officer, (St. George's Church,)
    41 Gordon's lane
Robertson, James, enterer, 108 George street

Entry	**Page 76**
1	*Will have some property at his mother's death, meantime a poor jobbing smith*
12[1]	*Widow of the most dashy baker in the town. Died in debt and had his splendid furniture rouped. Poor*
14	*Old man a famed operator in his day till within 5 years never sober now quite reformed and aided by his son is again recovering an excellent lost practice*
16[2]	*Long accountant in the Paisley Union. 1832, cashier of the Western's Branch there. 1834, agent for the Glasgow Union. 1839, Manager of the Paisley Commercial. A stiff overbearing tempered man*
17[3]	*Not wealthy, rather limited in means for the amount he does. And being an obligant in two bills of the community (£5,660) makes him dangerous. Was a magistrate last year*
18	*Are highly spoken of in Paisley, but are four miles from it. Old man died this year 1841 or last*
22	*Insolvent, composition 16/-. Pitied. Were not in the flash trade and had considerable means*
27[4]	*Borrowed on cautionry of friends in 1810 £60. Paid in 1816 £500 for property. Sold it in 1829 with large profit. Bought 1830 a valuable garden. Got last year £500 railway damage*
30[5]	*Has very considerable means left by the father 3 years ago. Are in a good business*

Robertson, James, farmer, Hillington
—Robertson, James, glass, china, and stoneware merchant, 86 High street, and 12 Wellmeadow—house do.
Robertson, James, hairdresser, 10 Lawn street
—Robertson, James, manufacturer, 92 Causeyside
Robertson, James, of Robertson, J. & J.—ho. 28 Storie st.
Robertson, James, warper, 13 Causeyside
Robertson, John, beamer, 18 Barclay street
Robertson, John, of Robertson, J. & J.—ho. 37 Canal st.
Robertson, John, spirit dealer, 12 High street
Robertson, John, theikar & feather dealer, 34 St. James' st.
—Robertson, John, wright, 19 Gauze street, and cowfeeder, 7 Inkle street
Robertson, Joseph, clerk at Donald & Craig's, 8 Renfrew street
Robertson, Joseph, grocer and spirit dealer, 35 Moss st. —house 4 Back Sneddon
—Robertson, Matthew, & Co. bleachers, Foxbar and Causey-end
Robertson, Mrs., midwife, 6 Wardrop street
Robertson, Mrs. Ross, Foxbar
—Robertson, Mrs. William, hatter, 97 High street
Robertson, Peter, reed maker, 98 Causeyside
Robertson, Quintin, dealer in simples and lash twines, 53 Storie street
Robertson, Robert, bugle tavern, 15 Moss street
Robertson, Robt., Govan coal agent, 19 Canal st.—house 75 do.
— Robertson, Robert, hat manufacturer, 1 High st.—ho. 77 do.
Robertson, Thomas, beamer, 2 Ferguslie
Robertson, Thomas, spirit dealer, 2 Dyer's wynd
Robertson, Thomas, of Foxbar
—Robertson, Walter, slater, 15 George street
Robertson, Wm., at Whyte, Jas., jun.—ho. 13 Wardrop st.
—Robin, D., and Co., manufacturers, 2 Forbes' place
Robin, David, of Robin, D., and Co.—house Saucel bank
Robinson, Nathaniel, excise officer—house Orchard st.
Rodger & Ferrie, silk and woollen dyers, 9 St. Mirren st.
— Rodger, Robert, of Wylie & Rodger—house Lonend
Ronald, David, flower lasher, 113 George street

Entry	**Page 77**
2	*Dead (November 1841) Has borne for 40 years a character of being comfortable, good business so long as Paisley could support a china shop. Has considerable property but is said to have died comparatively poor*
4	*Don't mistake him for No.5 [James]. No.4 poor as Lazerous. And tricky, not respectable*
5[1]	*[Blank, see above]*
11	*Had considerable means but was ruined by tax collector (Kerr) in 1835 paid 3/6 pr £, will never get on*
14	*Reported very wealthy, old established concern*
17[2]	*Her husband paid 5/- in 1828 widow and daughters done the best they can for a living. In a bad trade*
22	*Son of the above (18) [Peter]. Has unquestionably the best of the line in town <u>and said</u> to be <u>doing well</u>. Beware, his father in law J Fulton can assist him and is believed to do so at times*
26[3]	*Strange tricky character. Have nothing to do with in cash nor employment*
28	*Had 3 years ago £6,000 individually gave then by Municipal Clerk a small share (an eight) May have lost £3,000. Was <u>robbed</u> by a £700 purchase of Dicks 24 hours before they failed. Has a good business and judiciously scattered amongst his customers*
32	*Wealthy and best trade in town*

Ronald, Mrs. James, grocer and spirit dealer, 92 New
    Sneddon
Ronald, William, plasterer, 23 St. James' street
Rorrison, Mrs., dressmaker, 10 Maxwellton street
Ross, Alexander, of Ross and Duncan—house Abercorn
    place, 13 Niddry street
5—Ross & Duncan, thread manufacturers, Abercorn factory,
    6 Abercorn street
Ross, James, broker, 76 High street
Ross, James, cowfeeder, 18 George street
8—Ross, James, Golden Lion Inn, 11 High street
Ross, Jas., spinning master, Adelphi mill, 68 New Sneddon
Ross, Miss J., dressmaker, 6 Silk street
Ross, Mrs. John—house Abercorn place, 13 Niddry st.
12—Ross, Philip, teacher, 3 Lillias' wynd—ho. 65 Love st.
Rowan, Andrew, farmer, 20 Ferguslie
Rowan, Andrew, flesher, 26 Moss street
Rowan, James, spirit dealer, 1 Brown's lane
16—Rowan, Robert, flesher, 27 High street, and 1 New street
    —house 86 High street
Rowan, Robert, gardener, Underwood street
18—Rowat, Robert, shawl manufacturer, 1 Cumberland Court,
    110 Causeyside—ho. 12 Wardrop street
19—Roxburgh, Andrew, of Roxburgh, John, & Son—ho. 13
    George street
20—Roxburgh, John & Son, manufacturers, 168 George street
Roxburgh, John, of Roxburgh, John, & Son—house 167
    George street
22—Rule, John, baker, 32 Orchard street
Rule, Mrs. John, 13 Abbey street
24—Rule, Robert, silk and yarn merchant, 109 Causeyside—
    house 43 Oakshaw street
Russell, Alexander, beamer, 69 Love street
Russell, Andrew, beamer, 9 Gauze street
27—Russell, Jas., architect, Three Mile House, Glasgow road
Russell, James, of Russell & King—ho. 4 Clark's place
Russell, James, grocer and spirit dealer, 3 Lylesland
Russell, John, grocer, 11 Broomlands
31—Russell, John, shawl warehouse, 6 Smithhills
Russell, John, smith and farrier, 1 Williamsburgh

Entry	**Page 78**
5[1]	*Original Ross dead leaving considerable means, concern carried on by young Ross. Duncan (the brother in law) dreadfully dissipated and put out of business 5 years ago. Respectable, good business and certainly in easy circumstances*
8	*One of 6 brothers who were left by an uncle £1,000 each in the 2 per cents. Sold his for £600 and spent it. Has failed twice in the last 5 years. The whole of his brothers' money is gone, the most of it anticipated*
12	*An insipid dissipated – was an Elder in the Church and put out*
16	*Father died in 1829 leaving £6,000 to 4 children and widow. Died intestate. The old brother (a weak minded lad) took 2 fifths giving the other 3 (of which Robert was one) a fifth each. Has an excellent trade, the best in town and has improved his position*
18	*Has almost been driven out of trade these two years by want of profit. Bought Wm Galloway's property last year for an investment. Has considerable means Bank stock, house property &c &c*
19[2]	*[Blank but see 20]*
20[3]	*Failed and paid 5/- in 1827 again 9/- 1832 again offers 12/- 1841. December 1841 failed on composition and is sequestrated. Dangerous speculative fools. Has sometimes been worth several thousand pounds. His late partner says nine thousand 2 years ago*
22	*Very poor*
24	*Insolvent. Composition 5/6*
27	*Good head, able hands, but never sober*
31[4]	*Once a leading man in the trade. Now a poor half-witted silly body. A kind of runner of goods for the needy getting a precarious living*

Russell, John, teacher, Paisley educational association school, 12 Hunter street—ho. 4 Caledonia street
—Russell & King, dyers, 4 Clark's place, Seedhill
Russell, Miss, dressmaker, 103 High street
Russell, Mrs., dressmaker, 21 Sandholes
Russell, Robert, cowfeeder, 80 Canal street
—Russell, Robert & Sons, ham warehouse & spirit retailers, 21 Abbey close
Russell, Thomas, beamer, 13 West Buchanan street
—Russell, William, flesher, 19 Sandholes
Russell, Wm., foreman, Kerr's dyework, 6 Bladda—ho. Saucel

SANDY, John, boot and shoe maker, 4 Thread street
—Sacell Brewery Company, 9 Saucel
Saucel Distillery, King street, Saucel
Saucel Distillery spirit cellar, 70 Love street
Scadlock, George, pattern drawer, 3 Garthland street
—Scott, John, agent, Glasgow Union Bank, 109 High st.—house 1 Gauze street
Scott, John, jun., clerk Glasgow Union Bank, 109 High st.—ho. 1 Gauze street
—Scott, Matthew, manufacturer, 109 Causeyside—house 1 Great Hamilton street
—Scott, Robt. & Co., butter, egg, and bacon store, 10 Moss st.
—Scott, Robert, shawl manufacturer, 11 Wardrop street
Semple, David, of Anderson & Semple—ho. 68 High st.
—Semple, Hugh, grocer and spirit dealer, 75 High street
Semple, John, spirit dealer and fish merchant, 13 St. Mirren street
Semple, Mrs., grocer, 6 Seedhill
Semple, Wm., spirit dealer, 34 St. James' street
Shanks, Alex., gardener, West Crossflat, shop, 11 Smithhills
Shanks, Wm., (No. 1) U. S. C. officer, 1 Oakshaw st.
Shannon & M'Menamy, clothlappers, 105 Causeyside
Shannon, Mrs., milliner, 104 Causeyside
Sharp, Duncan, shoemaker, 11 Back Sneddon
Sharp, Miss, dressmaker, 4 Christie street
Sharp, Thos., of Brown, Sharps, & Co.—house 32 New st.

Entry	**Page 79**
2	*Have scarcely got a beginning. Both good tradesmen. Russell steady and with 2 or 400 pound saved by industry. King not so steady. Will not get on at this time, though abilities merit it*
6	*Strangers to Paisley. Do not give any symptoms of having means*
8	*Disreputable character*
11	*Chief partner dead (E B Buchannan) carried on by widow's executors and other partners – counted quite safe*
(12)	*See Stewart*
(13)	*Ditto*
15[1]	*A boy in the Paisley Union Bank then clerk, then (1810) accountant then (1815) cashier. Mild excellent business man and highly respected. Has personally considerable means got by savings and wife's legacies*
17[2]	*Insolvent. Industrious. Had made a little. Was finished by Dick*
18	*Poor. Was discovered lately to be a concern to draw on by a scoundrel in Cork, who has absconded. Beware*
19	*Insolvent. Gone to America after laying in jail 3 months*
21	*Has a good business, and money saved. Lent £250 to his brother No.20 to assist in building a large tenement this year. Cautious, safe. Had his money in Western Bank*
25	*Poor poor*
27[3]	*A dangerous character (Shannon) is in a new concern every 2nd year. The present company got up to prevent old creditors from interfering*
28	*His wife whose money he squandered away in foolish attempts to go into the grain trade*

Sharp, William, of Brown, Sharps, and Co.—ho. George place
Shaw, David, carter, Underwood lane
Shaw, John, baker, 32 Wellmeadow
Shaw, Robt., of Coats & Shaw—house 22 King street
Shaw, Robt., wine and spirit merchant, 82 Broomlands
Shaw, Robert, tailor, 18 High street
Shaw, William, fishmonger, &c., 41 Moss street
Shearer, Alex. & Co., furnishings, &c., 18 Causeyside
Shearer, John, wine and spirit dealer, 70 Broomlands
Shearer, Robt., & Co., shawl washers and scourers, Meikleriggs—general washing field
Shedden, John, merchant, 12 Causeyside
Shirlaw, Mrs., midwife, 26 Causeyside
Shirlaw, Thomas, wright, 2 Queen street
Shirlaw, William, hairdresser, 99 High street
Shute, Henry, barrack sergeant, barracks, Williamsburgh
Sim, Hugh, collector of statute labour money and prison assessment for Paisley, chamberlain's office, County Buildings
Sim, James, foreman to Carlile, James, & Son, 13 Carlile place
Sim, Matthew, spirit dealer, 22 Hamilton street, Calside
Sim, Simon, sen., baker, 6 Glen street
Sim, Wm., and Co., hard and soft soap manufacturers, 1 West Croft street
Sim, Wm., of Sim, Wm., and Co.—house Gallowhill
Simm, Robert, feuar, XXI. Wellmeadow street
Simpson, John, sacking & canvas manufacturer, 2 Cotton street—house do.
Simpson, John, wood turner, 85 High street—house Oakshaw street
Simpson, Mrs., milliner and dressmaker, 8 Moss street
Simpson, Peter, cowfeeder, 93 High street
Sinclair, Archd., hat maker, 94 High street—house do.
Sinclair, Archd., stoneware dealer, 118 George street
Sinclair, Daniel, shoemaker, 31 Cotton street
Sinclair, Hugh, shoemaker, 10 Silk street
Sinclair, James, salesman to Glen, Thomas, baker, 18 Broomlands

Entry	**Page 80**
5	*Married widow of late councillor Dunlop and a good business. Is the individual partner of Coats and Shaw. Insolvent, and must also be down on his spirit trade*
8	*Will have a triffle of property at his mother's death. Can be assisted by a maiden aunt, and must have been so – Beware of them Poor*
11	*Failed in 1822. Has since recovered a little. In a dangerous trade (supplying English drapers with Paisley shawls) Beware of him. Has the power of doing much mischief before being detected, but surely too honourable to do so*
13, 14	*[Thomas and William] Of long standing but poor*
19	*Good business and considerable house property. Has a ne'er-do-well family which has hurt him much cautiousness is requisite*
20	*The only partner a nephew who has been with him from infancy. Very wealthy. Has the command of the trade in the county. Has much valuable property – Purchased Gallowhill estate 1834. Has (1837) built a handsome mansion house on it*
22	*An Antiquary, hence the type*
27	*Old established trade. Has some property by heritage in Renfrew, and some which he built in Paisley. Safe*

Sinclair, John, jun., grocer, 3 Garthland street
Sinclair, John, sen., feuar, 2 Garthland street
—Skeoch, M., twine manufacturer, 16 Causeyside
Slater & Co., pawnbrokers, 20 Smithhills
Slater, David, warper, 20 Smithhills
Slater, John, of Haircraigs, farmer
—Slater, Matthew, starcher, 20 Smithhills—house 3 Great Hamilton street
—Slater, Peter F., draper, silk mercer, and straw hat manufacturer, 21 High street
Slevin, Dennis, broker, 10 Silk street
Sloan, James, spirit dealer, 5 Silk street
—Sloan, James, & Co , spirit dealers, 84 Causeyside
Sloan, Mrs., dressmaker, 8 New street
Small, John, broker, 12 Old Sneddon
Small, W. & J., bird stuffers, 4 Ganze street
Smellie, James, carrier, (Glasgow) 5 Abbey street
—Smith, Alex., wine & spirit merchant, 11 Dyer's wynd
Smith, Allan, librarian, Paisley trades' library, & teacher, 35 Canal street
—Smith, Andrew, coach builder and harness maker, 4 Garthland lane—house 3 do.
—Smith, Andrew, spirit dealer, 2 Bladda
—Smith, A. & W., & Co., mill wrights & machine makers, 9 William street
Smith & Co., clothlappers, 16 Causeyside
—Smith, Charles, grocer & spirit dealer, Carriagehill
Smith, David, farmer, Stirling street
Smith, David, feuar, 5 West Buchanan street
Smith, David, late merchant tailor, 5 West Buchanan st.
Smith, David, surveyor of stamps and taxes for Renfrewshire, Gilmour street—house 33 Oakshaw street
Smith, Elizabeth, crystal, china, and stone warehouse, 1 Broomlands
—Smith, George, brick & tile maker, Caledonia brickfield, Greenock road, and spirit dealer, Nethercommon
Smith, Hugh, wholesale and retail boot and shoe warehouse, 50 Moss street
Smith, James, coal merchant, 2 Hamilton st., Charleston
Smith, James, cork cutter, 12 New street

Entry	**Page 81**
3[1]	*Had 5 or 6 lands of houses left him by a brother in Kilbirnie and a little cash. Was ignorant of the town and gave credit freely. Has got the houses but must have contracted debt amongst his friends (who are said to be easy) to make up the great losses he has met with. All but ruined*
7[2]	*Has much property and respectable tenants but too much to be free. Must have a great surplus rental, being wealthy before he built in 1826. One of the magistrates involved in the town, to gratify his vanity but will not lack the amount. An excellent trade. An industrious labouring man*
8	*Son of the above with a little from his father. Will be driven out of the trade by the times. Only one year in it*
11	*Gone somewhere else – No business*
16	*Has a first rate ale house frequented by the better class of club attenders. Must in the past 10 years have done well*
18	*Insolvent. Composition 10/- never should have come to the town. One year in it*
19	*Thirty years standing. The house of call for the last 100 years for all the south east farmers. Making money and adding house to house periodically*
20	*[Blank]*
22	*Son of 18 [Robert] following page. Had a beginning from his father, and making money by sheer economy*
(23)	*Dead*
28	*Had means, but always in confusion and certainly some of these gone stands high in name. Beware of him*

Smith, James, flesher & ham curer, 94 High street
Smith, James, & Son, timber merchants, 72 New Sneddon—house 1 Carlile place
Smith, James, tailor, 31 Moss street
Smith, James, twister, 7 West Campbell street
Smith, John, grocer, 5 New Smithhills
Smith, John, leather cutter, boot and shoe maker, 2 Broomlands
Smith, John, pattern drawer & print cutter, 21 Gauze st.
Smith, John, spirit dealer, 22 Sandholes
Smith John, tailor, 99 High street
Smith, John, shawl merchant, 7 and 15 Causeyside—house Charleston cottage
Smith, Misses, straw hat and dress makers, 5 West Buchanan street
Smith, Mrs., eating house, 6 New street
Smith, Mrs., grocer, 86 Causeyside
Smith, Mrs. David, grocer, 1 Neilston street
Smith, Richmond, tailor, 16 High street
Smith, Robert, carter, 25 Lady lane
Smith, Robert, late auctioneer, 24 Broomlands
Smith, Robert, grocer, 12 Broomlands—ho. 4 William st.
Smith, Robert, jun., & Co., pawnbrokers, 7 Gauze street
Smith, Robert, & Co., pawnbrokers, 32 Gauze street
Smith, Robert, spirit merchant, 6 Smithhills, (carriers' quarters)
Smith, Thomas, tailor, 36 Moss street
Smith, William, feuar, 14 Ferguslie
Smith, Wm., of Gemmill & Smith—ho 26 High street
Smith, William, late spirit merchant, 4 Stow place
Smith, William, manufacturer, 15 Causeyside
Smith, William, tailor, 20 Causeyside
Sneddon Dispensary, William Cleland, 7 Old Sneddon
Snodgrass, J. & J., millers and grain merchants, Cardonald mill
Snodgrass, John, miller and grain dealer, 22 Seedhill—house 24 do.
Snodgrass, John, painter, oil & colour man, 1 High street—house 28 Gauze street
Snowdon, Rev. John, 65 Love street

Entry	**Page 82**
1	*Attempted to abscond this year but taken at Liverpool with £200 on him*
2	*Very wealthy, made offer of £13,000 for estate of Ranfurly in 1833. Have the complete command of the wood trade in Paisley. Have much property landed and in vessels*
10[1]	*One of the magistrates, but not involved, would not sign municipal bills to the community. Grants none himself. Has an excellent trade (cash) with Irish &c hawkers. Has much property bonded – and some purchased lately free. Is an altered man within these 5 or 6 years. Now quite safe*
(11)	*Industrious; have made money*
18	*Has property, clear, and a good trade*
19[2]	*Poor for the business must have some friend who supplies – not seen*
20	*Has means, are going to separate*
21	*Well-spoken of and said to have made during the last 10 years a little money*
26	*No trade. Merely a maker for his brother No.10 above. No means*
29, 30	*Looked upon as being people of means. Distant from town 3 miles and not well-known in it*
31[3]	*Best trade in the line, not wealthy but easy, and respectable*
32	*An itinerant Methodist of some knew [sic] connexion. A stranger*

Society Rooms, 22 Moss street—John Muir, clerk
Sommerville, Wm., boot and shoe maker, Lylesland
Sorbie, Mrs, dressmaker, 10 Old Sneddon
Southwell, Sam., flaxdresser and ropemaker, 18 High st.
Spiers, David, manufacturer, 4 Cumberland Court, 110 Causeyside—house 30 Orchard street
Spiers, Robert, turner, 11 Saucel
Spiers, Robert, R. N.—house 25 Glen street
Spence, John, butter & egg store, 14 Storie street
Spreul, James, veterinary surgeon, 8 Christie street
Spreul, Miss, dressmaker, 1 Wellmeadow
Spreul, Thomas, spirit dealer, 2 Broomlands
Sproul, Andrew, foreman at Lowndes, William & James, & Co.—house 49 Caledonia street
Sproul, James, broker, 10 Gauze street
Sproul, John, broker, 83 New Sneddon
Sproul, Robert, of Best & Sproul—house 8 Christie street
Stalker, John, dyer, 9 New Smithhills—house do.
Standford, William, hosier, 4 East Buchanan street
Steel, Robert, manufacturer, 52 Caledonia street
Steven, J. & W., patent rope work office, seeds, sheeting, &c., 82 High street
Steven, James, of Steven, J. & W.—ho. 23 Oakshaw st.
Steven, William, of Steven, J. & W.—ho. 58 Storie st.
Stevenson, James, seedsman and agent for London snuffs, 1 St. Mirren street—house 22 Smithhills
Stevenson, James, stoneware dealer, 169 George street
Stevenson, James, spirit dealer, 88 Canal street
Stevenson, John, accountant & measurer, 1 Bank street
Stevenson, John, spirit dealer, 36 Moss street
Stevenson, Miss, leghorn and straw hat maker, 121 George street
Stevenson, Mrs. Allan, spirit dealer and eating house, (Royal Oak Inn) 45 Moss street
Stevenson, Rev. Robert, 57 Love street
Stevenson, Robert, accountant, Glasgow Union Bank, 109 High street—ho. 28 New Smithhills
Stevenson, Robert, at Forbes, Chirney, & Hutchison— ho. 73 Causeyside

Entry	Page 83
5[1]	*Insolvent. Ought never to have been in trade*
6	*In a respectable trade of long standing.* <u>*Said to be easy*</u>
16	*Failed in 1826 or 7. Has since made money and purchased some property. Has quiet safe customers, will deal no others. In good credit & safe*
18	*Has no credit, No means. No trade. Has a house bonded to the full*
19	*The only respectable rope makers in town. Must have a little means are tired of the town and going to leave it. One of the brothers at America on the lookout for a better kingdom*
22	*Excellent trade, doing well and industrious very radical 10 years ago – much changed now – has made a little money*
28[2]	*From Johnstone 1834. Died 1838 supposed to be a poor widow*
29[3]	*A so so preacher Middle parish takes no public lead in anything. Has not the abilities they say*
30	*To the lips in poverty and embarrassment*

Stevenson, Thomas, letter-runner—ho. 14 Thread street
Steuart, Robert, of Steuarthall, sheriff clerk, County Buildings—residence Millburn House, Renfrew
Stewart, Alex., carding master, Underwood mill
Stewart, Allan, surgeon, 50 High street
Stewart, Allan, watchmaker, jeweller and hardware merchant, 92 High street—house 13 Barclay street
Stewart, Archd., late merchant—house 1 Christie st.
Stewart, Charles J. E., writing master, 7 Oakshaw st.
Stewart, David, thibet and shawl cutter, 28 Gordon's lane—ho. 26 Causeyside
Stewart, George, cutler and gunmaker, 89 High street
Stewart, James, Buck Head and tap room, 17 High st.
Stewart, James, distiller, King street, Saucel—ho. do.
Stewart, James, grocer and tea merchant, 17 Wellmeadow—house do.
Stewart, James, leather cutter, 3 New street
Stewart, James, superintendent of police, County Buildings—house 105 Causeyside
Stewart, James, superintendent of railway, Paisley station, Gilmour street—ho. 17 Wellmeadow
Stewart, John, feuar,—house Burns' place
Stewart, John, shawl washer, thibet scourer and stover, Arkleston field
Stewart, Matthew, starcher and bleacher, 48 Causeyside—general washing field
Stewart, Margaret, dressmaker, 15 Wellmeadow
Stewart, Miss, matron, House of Recovery, 11 Bridge st. (burgh)
Stewart, Mrs., broker, 81 Causeyside
Stewart, Mrs. Bryce, tinsmith, 1 Broomlands
Stewart, Mrs. Charles, spirit dealer, 74 Love street
Stewart, Mrs., Eagle Inn, (up 1 stair) 8 High street
Stewart, Mrs., midwife, 71 Broomlands
Stewart, Peter, flesher, 31 Causeyside
Stewart, Peter, manufacturer, 2 Canal street
Stewart, Robert, of Murray & Stewart—house, 69 High street
Stewart, Robert, grocer, 18 Lady lane
Stewart, Robert, tailor, 103 High street

Entry	**Page 84**
4[1]	*First rate business. Has acquired from 30 years' experience considerable property*
5	*Never pays his way. Insolvent every two or three years. Foolish trader*
6[2]	*Retired, very wealthy*
7	*Great grandson (natural) of the Pretender*
11	*Does very large business, too large for his means and manner of conducting it. Has now a young man (Mr Menzies) who is making great reformation in the manner of conducting the business, but could not add much means (if any). Beware*
12	*Insolvent. Sequestrated. Much pitied. A foolish extravagant wife the cause of the slippage and loss*
15[3]	*Same [person] as 12 [James]. Going to G & G Railway*
16[4]	*Retired wealthy, had about £10,000 left him. Had many years an excellent trade and good profits*
17	*Had much money and five years ago purchased some property with his spare means. Now (1841) evidently all gone and in poverty*
18	*His brother to whom the same character is applicable – Off to America*
24	*An industrious widow apparently doing well for the past 10 years. Is in an excellent situation and well frequented house*
26, 27[5]	*One person. Made a little money in a very disreputable way buying stolen weft &c. Always watched by the Police and sometimes fined. Has acquired a little property. Known by the tittle of "Duke Wellington"*

Stewart, Robert, warper, 8 Orchard street
Stewart, Thomas, keeper, Renfrew road toll bar
Stewart, Thomas, wright, 15 Wellmeadow
Stewart, Walter, Temperance Hotel and News Rooms, 19 Smithhills
Stewart, Walter, keeper East toll bar
Stewart, William, boot and shoe maker, 58 Storie street
Stewart, William, church officer, West Relief—house 3 Ralston square
Stewart, William, enterer, 148 George street
Stewart, William, pawnbroker, 2 South Croft street
Stewart, William, picking master, Adelphi mill, 68 New Sneddon
Stewart, William, tailor, 17 Causoyside
Stewart, William, teacher, 1 Bank st.—ho. 26 Lawn street
Stirling, Archibald, spirit dealer, 2 Millerston
Stirling, William & Co., saddlers, 89 High street
Stirrat, Jas., thread manufacturer, 61 High st.—bleacher, Nethercraigs, Abbey parish—house 10 West brae
Stoddard, David, shoemaker, 60 Back Sneddon
Storie, John P., of Riccartsbar
Stow, Misses, 5 Stow place
Struthers, James, farmer, Collinslee
Struthers, Thomas, farmer, South Gallowhill
Stuart, John, tailor, 6 Moss street
Stuart, Matthew, foreman at Carlile, James, & Son, 13 Carlile place
Sunter, Thomas, grocer and spirit dealer, 3 St. James' st.
Sutherland, Mrs., milliner & dressmaker, 97 Causeyside
Swainey, Hugh, weavers' furnishings, 16 Storie street
Swainey, John, broker, 28 Wellmeadow
Swainey, John, confectioner, 3 Wellmeadow
Swainey, Mrs., broker, 78 High street
Swainey, Thos., shoemaker, 48 Hamilton, st., Charleston
Swan, William, Fox tavern, 9 High street
Swanson, Mrs., straw hat maker, 9 St. James' place
Symington, George, ironmonger, 107 High street—house Saucel Bank
Symington, Mrs. Walter, hosier and draper, 10 High st.—house do.

Entry	**Page 85**
9	*Perhaps 4 or 500 pounds saved by industry and rigid economy and is making it more. Is a well doing man*
13	*Lives in his own property free. Has money besides. Has a good trade and a pension as [blank] in the Navey*
14	*Old name kept up Stirling died 1833. Trade purchased from widow by James King for his brother Thomas (since died) James King of Yardfoot, wealthy. Got a £1,000 railway damage for his farm this year*
15[1]	*Very considerable means and a good business. A town councillor but not involved. Quite safe. Heir to his uncle Robert Pattison page 70 [72] an old man & £15,000 or £18,000*
17[2]	*Heired £5,000 from his uncle – all spent – in poverty – nothing but the name*
20	*One of our best farmers, doing well*
32[3]	*Had a few hundreds from his father but with the rank he holds out it is astonishing it has lasted so long. Married expecting money but now disappointed daughter of [Thomas Gilmour] 25 page 40*
33[4]	*Insolvent at her husband's death 1833. Can have little or nothing but good friends assisting out of compassion*

1 Symington, R. B. & Co., manufacturers, 4 Cumberland Court, 110 Causeyside
2 Symington, Rev. Andrew, D.D., professor of divinity to the Reformed Synod—house 38 Oakshaw street
3 Symington, William, agent, 4 Cumberland Court, 110 Causeyside

TANNAHILL, Andrew, at Whyte, James, jun.—house 26 Glen street
Tannahill and Christie, shawl cutters and thibet croppers,
Tannahill, John, plaid and shawl shop, 1 Smithhills
Tannahill, J. and T., clothlappers, 12 Causeyside
Tannahill, John, of Tannahill, J. and T.—ho. 6 Barclay st. 28 Gordon's lane
9 —Tannahill, Thomas, late manufacturer, 13 West brae
Tannahill, Thomas, of Tannahill, J. and T.—house 23 St. James' street
11 —Tannock, James, victualler and spirit dealer, 6 Smith st.
Tannock, Matthew, flower lasher, 78 Canal street
Taylor, Alexander, pattern drawer, 113 Causeyside—house, 12 Saucel
14 —Taylor, George, (Terrace Tavern,) and machine maker, 5 Christie terrace
Taylor, James, librarian and newsman, 2 Christie terrace
16 —Tailor, James, tailor, 12 High street
17 —Taylor, John, boot and shoe maker, 23 High street
Taylor, John, warper, 13 Causeyside
Taylor, Miss M., milliner and straw hat maker, 9 Smithhills
Taylor, Robert, baker, 105 George street
Taylor, Robert, eating house, 6 New Smithhills
22 —Taylor, Thomas, and Co., manufacturers, 8 Causeyside—house 46 Oakshaw street
Taylor, Walter, grocer and spirit dealer, 6 Storie street
Taylor, William, foreman at Baird and Wallace—house 23 High street
25 —Taylor, William, writer—house 4 Garthland street
Teas, Andrew, grocer and spirit dealer, 36 Ferguslie
Teas, Joseph, broker & shoe maker, 4 New Smithhills
Telfer, David, letter-runner—house 3 Maxwell street

Entry	**Page 86**
1[1]	*Father dead but son carrying on an old established trade, not wealthy but respectable. Has not been hurt any this year*
3[2]	*Son of 2 [Andrew] who has perished the pack and left town*
9	*Retired, not wealthy but with a sum sufficient to keep him in his canny way*
11	*Insolvent to the surprise of everyone*
14	*A great trade, well-paying house scandalously taken in to 300 with Holms and Andrews by a kind lend 2 days before they failed. Has something left*
16[3]	*Old established but has not much money*
17	*Fails periodically. Had a windfall last year by a cousin dying suddenly intestate leaving him from £700 to £1,000*
22	*Wealthy. At times a large trade, all cash, and every scrabbling advantage taken of all whom money will tempt. Son Town Treasurer, involved £700 but it is nothing to him*
25	*Poor dissipated mortal*

Telfer, James, skinner, 7 New Smithhills
Telfer, Thomas, beamer, 78 Causeyside
Templeton, Andrew, & Co., saddlers, 80 High street
Templeton, John, tailor, 41 High street
Templeton, Wm., grocer and spirit dealer, 15 George st.
—Thomson, Alex., reedmaker, 12 Causeyside, and 116 do.
—Thomson, Andrew, manufacturer, 116 Causeyside—ho. 64 Broomlands
Thomson, Andrew, professor of music, 31 Gauze st.
Thomson, Andw., jun., professor of dancing, 31 Gauze st.
Thomson, David, sexton, 9 Oakshaw street
—Thomson, George, cotton yarn merchant, 9 Moss street —house 13 Old Sneddon
—Thomson, Hugh, ironmonger, 3 High street—house 9 Wellmeadow
—Thomson, J. T., feuar, 28 Millerston
—Thomson, James, grocer and spirit dealer, 42 Moss st.
—Thomson, James, brick builder and manufacturer of draining tile and bricks of all descriptions—brick work, East lane, 22 Williamsburgh—house 24 do.
—Thomson, John, accountant, 3 Moss street—ho. Blackland Cottage, Calside
—Thomson, John, jun., cloth merchant & hatter, 29 High street – house 45 New street
Thomson, John, of Gibb & Thomson—house Linside
– Thomson, John, sen., late merchant, 66 High street
Thomson, Miss Isabella, milliner and straw hat maker, 17 Storie street
Thomson, Mrs. David, 4 Garthland street
Thomson, Mrs. James—house 2 Garthland place
Thomson, Mrs. William, 21 Caledonia street
—Thomson, Robert, grocer, 26 Causeyside
Thomson, Robert, spirit dealer, 17 Moss street
Thomson, Thomas, flesher, 50 George street
Thomson, Thomas, and Co., grocers and spirit dealers, 29 Gauze street
—Thomson, Thomas, manufacturer, 6 George st.—ho. do.
—Thomson, Thomas, woollen manuf., Carriagehill factory
—Thomson, Wm., & Co., iron founders, 89 New Sneddon
—Thomson, William, manufacturer, 6 Barr street
Thomson, William, sheriff officer, 6 Moss street

Entry	**Page 87**
1[1]	*Considerable means both in property and Water, Bank shares &c. Adding house to house occasionally. Quite safe*
6	*Was left a little money some years ago which he is not spending nor improving*
7[2]	*The trade of the late James Muir sen. whose nephew he was. Could not have much means, nor never made anything. Beware of him*
11	*Insolvent. Brought down by Cooks*
12[3]	*Insolvent, composition 7/6. Had considerable means left by his father, but all went in a most mysterious way. Quite [?quiet] tippling*
13	*Gone to New York, but has left as much property as will pay his debts*
15[4]	*An industrious man. Is (owing to loss of £200 this year by Barr and Wallace) scarce of money but has a little yet to lose*
16	*Poor poor, once wealthy. His property all gone and little employment*
17[5], 19	*[John, jun. and John, sen.] Father and son, has much property of some kind in the family, left by a relation of old Mrs Thomson in which she is liferented. Both respectable. Leaving town said to be for Glasgow*
24	*A young beginner. Means unknown. His predecessor (to whom he was shopman) gave it up as not paying*
28[6], 29	*Insolvent 4 times. At this time standing still on composition of 9/- on £38,000. First instalment 3/- paid. A speculative fool*
30	*Failed 1829 paid 5/-. Laird the only surviving partner in 1840 died that year. The son still conducting the business. His success doubtful*
31[7]	*Scarcely deserves the name – does very little*

—Thompson, Joseph, yarn merchant, 26 Orchard street—house Ferguslie cottage
—Thompson, Mrs. George, 10 Gordon's lane
—Thompson, Mrs. John, 10 Gordon's lane
—Thompson, Thomas, leather merchant, 37 Gordon's lane
Thompson's tuscan, straw, and millinery warehouse, 88 High street
—Todd, George, tobacconist, 1 Moss st.—ho. Blackhall
Torbet, William, surgeon, 1 Lawn st.—ho. 27 Gauze st.
Torrance, David, salesman at Monkland coal wharf, 2 Carlile place—house 8 Wardrop street
Trades' Library, 42 New street
—Turiff, A. & Co., Vulcan foundry, 3 Abercorn st.—ho. 9 do.
—Turnbull & Bisset, jun., shawl warehouse, 3 Causeyside
Turnbull, George, victualler, 22 Sandholes
—Turnbull, James, baker, 78 Broomlands
—Turnbull, Mrs. James, sen., 4 Back row, Sandholes
Turner, Robert, feuar, 24 Oakshaw street
—Twigg, Joseph, cotton spinner, Adelphi mill, 68 New Sneddon—house Adelphi place, 41 New Sneddon
Twigg, Misses, boarding and day school, 34 Gauze st.
Twigg, Thomas, teacher, 5 Middle lane

—URIE & BROWN, shawl manufs., 113 Causeyside
Urie, Mrs. William, milliner, 86 High street
—Urie, Robert, baker, 73 Love street
Urie, Robert, of Urie & Brown—house 51 Broomlands
Urie, Wm., confectioner, 29 High street—house 86 do.

—VALLANCE, Alex., wright, 17 Moss street—ho. 36 do.
—Vallance, James, cabinet maker and furniture warehouse, 68 Broomlands—house do.
—Vallance, James, & Co., tobacconists, 8 High street (Cross)—house 41 Oakshaw street
—Vallance, John, wright and ironmonger, 26 George st.
Vallintine, John, tailor, 106 George street
—Vessie, William, surgeon and druggist, 9 St. James' place—house do.

WADE, Misses, boarding and day school for young ladies, 34 Moss street

Entry	**Page 88**
1	*Poor poor, gone to London for employment*
2[1], 3	*Two wealthy widows, sisters in law to 4 [Thomas]*
4[2]	*Very wealthy and making daily more. Has large sums sunk in mortgage Pollock & Gilmour has £700 bond from him. The bond was in the property when P & G had to take it as creditors of Knox in 1822. Thomson will not take payment*
5[3]	*Daughter of 19 [John Thomson sen.] prior page*
6[4]	*Wealthy. One of our magistrates. Owed along with 11 others in £6,800 accommodation bills to the town. His share will not be felt to him. Excellent business. Shrewd man. His municipal vanity has overcome him*
10	*Respectable company – Reid & Hanna – A Fullerton and others partners – [crossing out]*
11	*Turnbull insolvent individually. The concern as a matter of course stand still*
13[5]	*Good trade, well doing and cautious, left considerable property by his father in 1836 and has improved it*
16[6]	*Paid 12/- in 1828. Borrowed £8,000 on mill and houses to pay it. Considerable reversion supposed to be left. Style of living too high and can have been doing no good of late*
19	*Insolvent – December. Stopped on composition*
21[7]	*Good trade. Industrious and some means*
24	*Poor industrious man*
25	*A good business, and considerable house property some of which is not bonded, but has suffered considerably at this time and will probably have to bond a little more to relieve himself*
26	*Father died November 1834 Only son succeeded to property trade &c reckoned at £20,000. Has married (1840) wife with several thousands*
27	*John Vallance paid 5/- in 1829 that year produced failures of a large circle of wrights all joined in accommodations none of which got on. Vallance one [of] them and very poor still – has a little well paid surplus lent over interest of bonds*
29[8]	*[Blank]*

Wade, Rev. W. M., clergyman of Trinity chapel—house 85 New Sneddon, and teacher of the English and French languages
—Walker, Alexander, baker, 41 Broomlands
Walker, Alexander, cowfeeder, 14 High street
Walker, David, grocer, Carriagehill
Walker, Hugh, spirit dealer, 16 Broomlands
Walker, James, boot and shoe maker, 71 Canal street
Walker, James M., eating house, 34 Old Sneddon
Walker, John, of Walker, Son, & Co.—house Greenside cottage, Calside
Walker, John, pattern drawer, at Baird & Wallace—ho. 74 Love street
Walker, John, jun., of Whitehill, M., & Co.—ho. Greenside cottage, Calside
—Walker, Mrs. John, cooper, 9 Moss street
—Walker, Mrs. William, feuar, 57 Canal street
Walker, Neil, tailor, 24 Lawn street
Walker, Robert, reedmaker, 27 New street
—Walker, Son, & Co., manufacturers, 113 Causeyside
—Walker, W. & R., timber merchants and wrights, 1 Abercorn street
Walker, William, tailor, Lylesland
Walkinshaw, Miss, 1 Christie street
Wallace, Alexander, slater, 11 Prussia street
Wallace, Charles, slater, 6 Smithhills—slate yard, 22 New Smithhills
—Wallace ● Connell, plumbers, Gilmour street, James Dalrymple, foreman—house 14 Back Sneddon
—Wallace, Hugh, manuf., 21 Causeyside—house Blackhall
Wallace, James, of Baird & Wallace—ho. 2 St. James' street
—Wallace, James, spirit dealer, 57 New Sneddon, and coal merchant, 30 New
—Wallace, John, grocer and spirit dealer, 56 George street
Wallace, John, pattern drawer, at Baird & Wallace—house 74 Love street
Wallace, John, spirit dealer, 92 Causeyside
Wallace, John, teacher, 34 Hamilton street
Wallace, Matthew, eating house, 32 Storie street

Entry	**Page 89**
2	*Has considerable means in trade and some excellent house property. Has a good business and highly reputable*
11[1]	*Husband drank himself to death the widow an industrious woman making a living but poor*
12	*As executrix for her husband who died 1835 took at the sight of arbiters £3,300 from the concern of Galloway & Walker. Has purchased house property*
15[2]	*Wealthy in their line and respected. The brother who formed Galloway & Walker in 1832 took £2,000 out of the concern as his share Have made money since*
16	*Highly respected <u>and said</u> to be in very excellent circumstances*
21	*Are poor. Was Orr & Wallace then widow only and now Wallace & Connell. Too many shiftings and little business*
22	*Insolvent. Composition 3/- ruined by [?]Wingate*
24	*Insolvent. Composition 6/8. Has lost a good heritage left by his father*
25	*Has had one of the best houses of this line in the town for many years, but is, to the wonder of all who know him, in abject poverty*

1 —Wallace, Matthew, & Co. coal and iron wharf, Carlile lane, 85 New Sneddon
2 —Wallace, Matthew, dyer, 56 New Sneddon—ho. 3 Glen st.
3 —Wallace, Robt., wine and spirit mercht., 3 Silk st.—ho. do.
Wallace, Samuel, coal agent, 5 Lawn street
Wallace, William, clothlapper, 3 Cumberland court, 110 Causeyside—house 10 Wardrop street
Wallace, William, eating house, 13 Gauze street
Wallace, William, grocer and spirit dealer, Carriagehill
Wallace, William, slater, 25 Lawn street
Wallace, William, wright and glazier, 80 Broomlands
Walls, John, broker, 43 Wellmeadow
Wands, James, cowfeeder, 68 Love street
Ward, John, clothier and tailor, 18 Moss street
Ward, John, tailor, 10 Castle st.
14 —Wardrop, Alex., manufacturer, 9 Wallace street
Wardrop, Mrs., furnished lodgings, 27 New Sneddon
16 —Wark, James, of Wark, Leckie, & Co.—house Lonend
17 —Wark, Leckie, & Co., dyers, Lonend dye works, Lonend
Wark, William, shoemaker and broker, 36 Moss street
19 —Warnock, Andw., cotton shag manufacturer, 59 High st.
Warrington, Miss, milliner and dressmaker, 14 St. James' place
Warrington, Samuel, pawnbroker, 9 Moss st.—house 14 St. James' place
22 —Warrington, Wm., pawnbroker, 9 Moss street—ho 25 do.
Waterston, Jas., painter, 45 High st., shop 7 Moss st.
Waterston, James, oil and colour merchant, 1 Moss street—house 6 Garthland street
Waterston, John, seedsman and florist, 45 High street
Watson, Archibald, spirit dealer, 21 Old Sneddon
Watson, Dewar, of Harvey, James & Co.—house 3 Churchhill
Watson, James, manager, power loom factory, 15 Abbey close—house 1 Ellis' lane
Watson, James, hairdresser, 72 Causeyside
30 —Watson, James, wine and spirit merchant, (tea gardens and bowling green,) 37 Causeyside
Watson, John, general grocer, 19 Orchard street
Watson, Mrs. James, cowfeeder, Carriagehill

Entry	**Page 90**
1, 2[1]	*[Matthew and Matthew above] are the same and a brother of 24 [James] prior page and in the same circumstances*
3	*Excellent business, has made money by it, and acquired some property. His wife has considerable means in fee but her mother liferented*
14	*Was (1818) the leading man of the town. Is a fool, and as poor as Lazerous. His mother has some property deeply bonded to G F Society*[a]
16	*Had £600 in 1830 which formed the capital of Wark, Leckie & Co. at that time. Left by father in law*
17	*Commenced in 1830 Wark with £600. Leckie a first rate tradesman – Hannah the 3rd partner, a good procurer of work Did well, the writer – Hannah's factor – got in 1838 Hannah's share for his widow £800. Have met with considerable loses at this time but not to cripple them*
19[2]	*Left £3,000 by his father in 1812, lost it nearly all in 1816 by New York speculation. Has made it nearly up again. Had wife's portion £600 added in 1830. Has considerable property in Australia and two sons managing there his farms and doing well. Has a good business here and no opposition*
22[3]	*Trustworthy. Bought a good tenement this year and as yet (Dec. 31) has no bond and does not intend to have. Though he has hampered his business beyond his intention*
30	*Was left considerable means lately. The writer presented a forged bill to him lately when he declared that his name had not been on a bill for several years*

---

[a] 'G F Society' may be Good Fellows Society

PAISLEY. 91

Watson, Mrs., milliner and dressmaker, 24 Gauze street
Watson, M., staymaker, 35 Causeyside
—Watson, P. & T., clothiers and hatters, 11 High street
—house 21 Caledonia street.
—Watson, W. & R., shawl manufacturers, 169 George st.
—Watt, John, wright and feuar, 2 Wallneuk
—Webster, William, grocer, spirit dealer, and flesher, 1 East Buchanan street
—Weddell, James, & Co., confectioners, 5 Moss street
Weir, Andrew, feuar, grocer, and spirit merchant, Weir's place, 33 Williamsburgh
—Weir, Archibald, merchant, 56 Causeyside
—Weir, Archibald, pastry baker, 33 Causeyside
Weir, John, grocer and spirit dealer, 4 Thread street
Weir, Mrs., grocer, 20 Gauze street
Weir, Robert, porter, (No. 1) 20 Glen street
—Weir, Wm., wine and spirit merchant, 3 Orchard street
—Welsh, Arthur, agent, British Linen Company's Bank —house 5 Bank street
Welsh, William, smith and farrier, Lonend
—White, George, & Co., manuf., 3 Cumberland court, 110 Causeyside
White, James, spirit dealer, 8 High street
White, John, farmer, Fulwood
White, Miss Ann, dressmaker, 27 Thread street
White, Misses, 30 Cotton street
White, William, farmer, Fulwood
White, Robert, farmer and cowfeeder, Maxwellton road, Calside
—Whiteford, Andrew, tailor, 28 Maxwellton street
—Whitehead, Joseph, & Son, tanners, 1 Seedhill
Whitehead, Joseph, of Whitehead, Joseph, & Son—ho. Kilnside House
—Whitehead, Misses, 14 Abbey street
Whitehill, Alexander, at Ferguson & Watson's—house 9 Wellmeadow
Whitehill, Mary, mangler, 8 Smithhills
—Whitehill, M., & Co., shawl merchants, 113 Causeyside
Whitehill, M., of Whitehill, M., & Co.—house 9 Wellmeadow

Entry	**Page 91**
3	*Said, by Dewar Watson, to take the discount at all settlements. Had accommodation from Bank of Scotland (by bill at 12 months) for £1,000 secured by 8 page 60 and the brother DW who is married on Muir's sister. The present crisis has caused the bill to be called up and it is paid. Give credit freely and make dreadful bad debts. May have done well enough but the writer is sceptical of the reported amount of property – Be Cautious*
4	*Insolvent under Trust*
5	*Lay long in jail lately defying his creditors with some property the tittles of which were in confusion, and beat them off. Avoid him*
6	*[Blank]*
7[1]	*Wealthy Has an excellent business. Has, this year, purchased valuable property at Cross, purely as an investment*
9[2]	*An old decayed manufacturer – failed*
10	*An old man with a triffling trade and his kitchen his sale room*
14	*Has an excellent business, about the best in the line. Has some means. A few hundred pounds lent in bond over what is employed in the trade*
15[3]	*Came in 1828 from Castle Douglas. Is not calculated for a <u>City Cashier</u>. Is passionate and, in good times, offends good customers. Is commonly named the "Old Schoolmaster" from his too great readiness to give instructions*
17	*Only a few months in business. Has no means*
24	*Poor poor behind with his rent*
25[4]	*Supposed the wealthiest in Renfrewshire*
27	*Wealthy old ladies. Antiquated said to have (with 25) of family money nearly half a million in the funds. Mr Millar writer, says £300,000*
30	*Young men of one year's standing with but triffling means from their father 28 say £300 or so. It is the surprise of every one that they are standing it out*

1 —Whyte, Andrew, feuar, 16 Stevenson street
Whyte, Charles, broker, 34 Causeyside
Whyte, James, colourmaker, printworks, Nethercommon
4 —Whyte, James, jun , manufacturer, 66 Back Sneddon— house Abbot's Burn, near Merksworth
5 —Whyte, James, shawl washer and general washing field, Shawfield
Whyte, James, flower lasher, 85 Causeyside
7 —Whyte, John, sen., manufacturer, 80 High street
8 —Whyte, John, jun., silk and cotton yarn warehouse, 13 Causeyside—house 93 New Sneddon
Whyte, Misses, boarding school for young ladies, 85 High st.
Whyte, Misses, milliners & straw hat makers, 54 High st.
Whyte, Miss Margaret, furnishing shop, 20 Gauze street
Whyte, Mrs., straw hat maker, 26 New Smithhills
Whyte, Neil, bill poster, 23 High street
14 —Whyte, Robert, manufacturer, 13 Old Sneddon
15 —Whyte, Robert, spirit dealer, 19 Causeyside, (carriers' quarters)
16 —Whyte, William, bleacher and shawl washer, Greenlaw bleachfield
Whyte, William, carter, 13 Sir Michael street
18 —Wight, Robt., grocer and spirit dealer, 4 South Croft st.
Wilkie, Andw., shuttle maker, 39 High st., & 62 Storie st.
Wilkie, James, painter, 39 High street, and 62 Storie st. —house 39 High street
21 —Wills, James, grocer and spirit dealer, 63 George street
Williamson, William, broker and weaving utensils, 10 New Smithhills
23 —Wilson, Alexander, grocer, 28 George street
Wilson, Andrew, of Wilson & Robertson—ho. 52 High st.
24—Wilson, James, grocer and spirit dealer, 20 George st.
25—Wilson, James, sen., grocer and vintner, 42 Broomlands
Wilson, Jean, grocer and spirit dealer, 5 Abbey close
27 Wilson, John—Ferguslie House *Dearly*
Wilson, John, feuar, 34 Oakshaw street
Wilson, John, & Sons, Hurlet—office, 5 Christie terrace, open on Thursdays from 10 till 4
Wilson, John, surgeon, 13 Broomlands
31 —Wilson, J., & Co., wine and spirit merchants, 17 Smithhills

Entry	Page 92
1[1]	Has a little property but went beyond his means, and having bad rented mostly tradesmen's houses is in difficulties
4[2]	Insolvent. Composition 11/-
5[3]	Poor poor
7[4]	Poor poor and plausibly dangerous, avoid him. Nickname "Dirty Whyte"
8	Insolvent. Composition 2/- and again failed on composition
14	Poor poor Brother of 4 [James jun.] above and must come down soon
15	Should do well. Has a well-paying house which he got by the death of a sister who made a little money in it
16[5]	Poor and dissipated
18	Has a good small trade in a good corner of the town and always a little money in the Bank
21	Insolvent. Composition 3/- brought down by James Loudon, otherwise solvent
23, 24, 25[6]	[Alexander, James and James sen.] Father and sons – Have means and all good businesses – The father said to have made considerable. Are undoubtedly easy in their business
27	Dead
31	Was blown up by the Earl Gray steam vessell and killed.[a] The widow left with free shop and otherwise easy

---

[a] The steamer *Earl Grey* plied between Rothesay, Dunoon, Greenock and Glasgow. On the evening of Friday 24th July 1835, while at berth in Greenock, her boiler exploded, killing 10 people on the boat and ashore, including John Wilson who died the following day. It was rumoured that the *Earl Grey* had been racing with another steamship, and her engineer, Hugh Davidson, was charged with culpable homicide, but found not guilty at the Circuit Court in Glasgow on 10th September 1835. See Paisley Advertiser, Saturday 25th July 1835, p. 1; ibid., Saturday 1st August 1835, p. 1; and ibid., Saturday 12th September 1835, p. 1

Wilson, Joseph, grocer and victualler, 24 Gordon's lane
Wilson, Margaret, grocer, 9 New Sneddon
—Wilson, Mary, spirit dealer, 16 Causeyside
Wilson, Miss, 4 Garthland street
Wilson, Miss, mangler, 1 Storie street
Wilson, Mrs., dressmaker, 13 Canal street
Wilson, Mrs. John, mangler, 11 Wellmeadow
Wilson, Mrs., furnishing shop, 70 High street
Wilson, Mrs. Robert, late tea dealer, 87 High street
Wilson, Peter, gardener, Crossflat
Wilson, Robert, of Barr & Wilson—house 7 Stow street
Wilson, Robert, of Lang & Wilson—house 34 High st.
—Wilson & Robertson, wholesale grain and provision merchants, 60 High street, and victuallers, 23 Gauze street, and 25 Moss street
Wilson, Thomas, druggist, 48 Moss street—ho. 39 New st.
Wilson, Thomas, shoemaker, 101 Causeyside
Wilson, Walter, keeper Exchange Rooms, 48 Moss st., and Renfrewshire Tontine Assembly Rooms, 1 Bank street—house 1 Dyer's wynd
Wilson, Wm., grocer, carter, and cowfeeder, 60 Canal st.
Wilson, William, warper, 17 Causeyside
—Wilson, William, shawl manufacturer, 5 Cumberland court, 110 Causeyside—house 34 Glen street
—Winning, James, flesher and ham curer, 61 Causeyside—house 59 do.
Winning, James, house factor, 5 Smith street
Woodrow, James, heddle dresser, 99 Causeyside
Woodrow, John, grocer, 37 Thread street
—Wotherspoon, Francis, merchant, Nitshill
—Wotherspoon, John, Eastern Apothecary Hall, 10 Smithhills—house 12 Barclay street
—Wotherspoon, W. & J., wholesale druggists and stationers, 4 Moss st., and 106 Cross, entry 1 Lillias' wynd
Wright, Daniel, eating house, 11 Smithhills
Wright, Daniel, flesher, 47 Moss st.—ho. 22 School wynd
—Wright, Daniel, & Son, spirit dealers and eating house, 17 Causeyside, (Kilbarchan carrier's quarters)
Wright, Daniel, victualler, 28 New Smithhills
Wright, Gillies, warper, 13 Causeyside

Entry	**Page 93**
3	*Poor poor changes her place every 2nd year*
13	*Commenced about 3 years ago, Wilson in a small way in the line means unknown, Robertson known to have nothing. Are reputed occasionally to be bankrupt but which has not taken place. Are highly dangerous – too extensive*
19[1]	*A well doing man commenced in May 1841 with but very limited means, succeeded his master James Porter who retired wealthy, and got a cheap and easy possession of his business. Has made (not being in time) no bad debts at this crisis and is likely to do well. Is obtaining regular credit*
20	*Poor Is leaving the town. Has opened a shop High street Glasgow*
24[2]	*Has acquired about £2,000 of good property in Paisley. No bonds*
25	*Youngest son of 24 with support from his father, Newly commenced*
26	*Elder sons of 24 supported by their father. Are industrious and taking a lead in their line of business*
27, 28, 29, 30	*[Daniel, Daniel, Daniel & Son and Daniel] Father, son & nephew, all poor. Father failed about 1828. Has done no good since*

Wright, James, tailor, 88 New Sneddon
Wright, John, gardener, 4 East Croft street
Wright, Miss Ellen, straw hat maker, 102 Causeyside
Wright, Mrs., dressmaker, 19 Newton street
Wright, Mrs., milliner & straw hat maker, 12 Smithhills
Wright, Peter, stocking maker, 17 Inkle street
Wright, Thos., late hair cutter and perfumer, 91 High st.
Wright, Walter, hair dresser, 10 Broomlands
Wright, Walter, hair dresser, 35 Ferguslie
Wright, William, grocer, 27 New Sneddon
Wright, William, hair dresser, 23 Abbey street
Wylde, Roger, & Son, manufacturers, 2 Cumberland Court, 110 Causeyside
Wylde, Roger, of Wylde, Roger, & Son—ho. 82 High street
Wylde, Thomas, of Wylde, Roger, & Son, house 65 Back Sneddon
Wylie, David, jun., & Co., glass and stone warehouse, 66 High street
Wylie, George, M. D. 9 Orr square
Wylie, James, wine and spirit merchant, 8 Wardrop st. —house do.
Wylie, John, flesher, 13 Broomlands
Wylie, John, & Co., pawnbrokers, 3 Orchard street
Wylie, Matthew, flesher, 26 Causeyside
Wylie, Mrs., cowfeeder, 23 Abbey street
Wylie, Mrs. Matthew, flesh shop, 83 Causeyside
Wylie, Mrs., milliner and dressmaker—109 George street
Wylie, Mrs. William, 13 Thread street
Wylie, Robert, of Wylie & Rodger—ho. 1 Garthland place
Wylie & Rodger, writers, 2 Lawn street
Wylie, Thomas, & Co., manufacturers, 4 South Croft st.
Wylie, Thomas, public servant, 15 Gordon's lane
Wylie, Wm., singeing house, 16 Causeyside—house 25 Orchard street
Wylie, William, victualler, 15 Old Sneddon

YOUNG, Andrew, boot and shoe maker, 18 High st. —house 9 School wynd
Young, Andrew, cowfeeder, 5 Wellmeadow
Young, Andrew, feuar, 7 Old Sneddon

Entry	**Page 94**
7[1]	Has left 2 to £3,000 mostly in property. His widow and shopman still carry on the business
8, 9, 10, 11	[Walter, Walter, William and William] Sons and grandsons of a famed hairdresser in the west end of Paisley who left a little property amongst them, which is mostly gone
12	The only remaining house in the Muslin trade left in town. Old established trade. Are in undoubted credit and are supposed to have made some wealth. Highly respectable
16[2]	Tolerable practice of the second class of shop keeper &c, and long in the profession
17	Long in the line. Has a cheap over counter trade. Must have suffered greatly of late. Had no capital at commencement
19[3]	Are too poor to be in the line
20	Poor, always in difficulties
21	Ditto
22[4]	Ditto, Mother of 20 [Matthew]
25[5]	Wealthy. The last survivor of 3 brothers who were all wealthy
26	By far the best business in town
27	No means. No credit. No trade they should not have a place in the directory
31	Long in the line and has always paid his way. Was an elder in the Establishment [Church] but gave it up last year
33	Very poor. Has a small property – bad rents

Young, D., & Co., tea merchants, 1 Christie terrace, & 26 Wellmeadow
Young, D., of Young, D., & Co.—house 3 Bladda
Young, George, feuar, spirit dealer, and thread manufacturer, 3 Love street
Young, George, plasterer—house 4 Glen street
Young, Homer, potato dealer, Newland Craig
Young, James, boot and shoe maker, and spirit dealer, 70 George street
Young, James, grocer & cowfeeder, 19 Cotton street
Young, James, grocer & spirit dealer, 10 New Sneddon
Young, John, foreman at Coats, J. & P.—house 6 Back row, Ferguslie
Young, John, foreman, Nethercraigs
Young, John, spirit dealer, 15 Thread street
Young, Miss M., dressmaker, 25 Glen street
Young, Mrs. Alex., milliner and straw hat maker, 6 Broomlands
Young, Mrs., furnished lodgings, 49 High street
Young, Mrs. George, 5 Glen street
Young, Mrs. James, feuar, 39 Canal street
Young, Rev. John, house 17 Back Sneddon
Young, Robert, foreman at Lowndes, William & James & Co.—ho. 25 Glen street
Young, Robert, Friendly Society officer, 122, George st.
Young, Robert, pattern drawer, 23 George street
Young, Robert, teacher, Sessional school, 125 George st.—house 57 Canal street
Young, Thomas, cabinet and chair maker, 16 High st.
Young, William, carter and cowfeeder, 3 Burn row
Young, William, manufacturer, 3 Old Sneddon
Young, William, manufacturer, 24 Orchard street—house 2 Garthland place
Yuill, James, farmer, Blackhall
Yuill, John, house surgeon and apothecary, House of Recovery, 11 Bridge street (burgh)
Yuill, Wm., grain, spirit dealer, & flesher, 11 St. James' place—gigs and saddle horses to hire

Entry	**Page 95**
1	*A set up of some Glasgow company unknown in Paisley. A Dash*
4	*Extremely dissipated. Has lost a good trade left him by his father and at his mother's death (Mrs George) will soon finish all*
(14)	*Dead*
15	*Mother of George Has considerable house property but will die poor. Horrid family*
17	*Separated from English Independents (now J McLauchland) and leads some 10 or 12 in a way of his own. A serious silly old man*
24	*A fool. Often in jail*
25	*Wealthy. Has good property bought merely for investment. Almost no business of late years*
26	*Reported easy. Industrious and respected*
28[1]	*Tricky strange character known by "Proddy Yuill". To be avoided on several accounts, though not altogether on the score of poverty*

APPENDIX I

From the 1847 *Topographical Dictionary* by Samuel Lewis.

PAISLEY

The Town is pleasantly situated on the White Cart, by which it is divided into two portions called respectively the Old and the New Town, the former on the west, and the latter on the eastern bank of that river. It consists principally of two streets intersecting each other at right angles; the one, nearly two miles in length, forms part of the road from Glasgow to Beith and the Ayrshire coast, and the other is a continuation of the road from Inchinnan to Neilston. These two lines are crossed in various directions by numerous spacious and well-built streets, of which George street and Forbes street contain many very handsome houses. The appearance of the town has been much improved by the removal of numbers of the older houses, and the most recent additions, Garthland Place, at the eastern entrance to Paisley, is distinguished as one of the most elegant ranges of building in this part of the country.

The streets are lighted with gas by a company incorporated in 1823, who embarked a capital of £16,000, and erected very extensive works for the supply of the neighbourhood. The inhabitants were till lately but indifferently furnished with water from the river, and from private and public wells. A company was therefore formed in 1835, for bringing water from the Gleniffer hills, and a capital of £40,000 subscribed, and two very capacious reservoirs [Stanely and Harelaw], covering nearly 100 acres, and having an average depth of almost 40 feet, have been constructed, furnishing an abundant supply of pure water for use of the inhabitants, and of the different public works carried on in the vicinity.

There is a public library, supported by subscription of about 200 proprietary shareholders; it comprises more than 4,500 volumes in the various departments of literature. In the town is also a very extensive library containing several thousand volumes, maintained by subscription of the operative classes; a library annexed to the Faculty of Procurators has a large collection of the most approved law books; and a medical library is attached to the House of Recovery, under the management of the Medical Society.

APPENDIX I

One newspaper is published weekly. The Philosophical Institution was established in 1808, for promoting the study of natural philosophy, general literature, and science, by the delivery of single lectures by the members gratuitously, and occasionally courses of lectures by eminent professors. Connected with it are a library of above 500 volumes, and a museum containing a very valuable collection of minerals and natural curiosities.

These are also some curiosities in the pleasant gardens in the immediate vicinity of the town called Hope Temple, comprising several acres of ground tastefully laid out, and forming an interesting place of resort to the inhabitants. To the east of the town, in the suburb of Williamsburgh, some very commodious barracks have been erected within the last 30 years; they are pleasantly situated and adapted to the reception of half a regiment of infantry.

The almost unequalled increase in the extent and population of Paisley, which formerly consisted only of one street, and contained scarcely 2,000 inhabitants, is to be attributed to the introduction of the various MANUFACTURES of which it is the seat, and for which its situation near the river Clyde, affording great facility of communication, renders it peculiarly favourable.

Not long after the union of the two kingdoms, when a free trade was opened, the few articles manufactured here, principally coarse checker *linens* and *Bengals*, were purchased by pedlars from England, who, selling them among their friends at home to advantage, regularly frequented this town as the principal mart, and, after acquiring some little property as itinerant merchants, took up their abode in Paisley, and became factors for supplying their correspondents in the south. The impetus thus given to the manufactures soon excited the attention of the Glasgow merchants, who bought large quantities, which they sent to London and to foreign markets. The manufacture of checked linen handkerchiefs, of different colours tastefully blended, was soon added to the articles previously made; and to these succeeded various fabrics of lighter texture, consisting chiefly of plain and figured *lawns*, and a new sort of sewing-thread, known by the appellation of *ounce* or *nuns'* thread, to distinguish it from other kinds manufactured at Aberdeen and Dundee. The manufacture of silk gauze, in imitation of that of Spitalfields, London, was introduced here about the year

1760, and was carried on with such success, and in such a variety of elegant patterns, as totally to supersede the making of that article by the London weavers. It soon became the staple manufacture of the place, and several companies from London settled in the town for the purpose of conducting it on a more extensive scale; it furnished employment to numbers of persons in the surrounding district for almost twenty miles, and the different manufactures here had agents for the sale of it in London, Dublin, Paris, and other parts of the continent. This manufacture, however, after a period of unexampled success for nearly thirty years, declined with the change of fashion, and was almost immediately succeeded by that of *muslin*, which was carried on by the same parties with much spirit and perseverance, and soon rose to a great degree of prosperity. The working of muslins with *embroidery* shortly followed; it was pursued with only moderate success for some time, but has been rapidly increasing within the last twenty years, and now gives employment to thousands of females in this widely extended manufacturing district. The value of the silk and linen gauze, and white sewing thread manufactured here in 1784, has been estimated at £579,185; and about 1790, the aggregate amount of all goods of every kind manufactured annually was computed at £660,385. The number of persons employed in 1784 in the gauze and thread works was 27,484. From the reports of the Board of Trustees for the encouragement of manufactures, it appears that the linen trade had in 1784 reached its greatest height; the number of looms that year was 2,000, and nearly 2,000,000 of yards were stamped [recorded for tax purposes]. About 5,000 looms were then, according the same authority, employed in the silk gauze manufacture, and the quantity produced was estimated at £350,000.

At the beginning of the 19th century, the manufacture of SHAWLS in imitation of those of India was attempted, at first only with comparatively moderate success; but by the perseverance and ingenuity of the persons embarked in it, the manufacture at length succeeded even beyond expectation, and shawls of soft and spun silk, and of cotton, were produced of admirable quality.

Imitations, also, of the scarfs and turbans worn by the eastern nations were made, and exported in great quantities to the islands of the Archipelago and to Turkey; and the same style of work was introduced in several varieties for ladies' dresses. This trade flourished for a long time, affording employment to great numbers of persons; and is still carried on to a considerable extent. A more perfect imitations of the Indian shawl was eventually obtained, by mixing fine wool and silk in the production of what was called Persian yarn; and a still nearer approximation was made by the introduction of the fabric called Thibet, originally manufacturers in Yorkshire, but afterwards adopted with improvements by the weavers of this place. The manufacture was at length brought to its present state of perfection by the use of cashmere wool from the east; this had been imported for some time by the French; and by obtaining yard from France, the Paisley manufacturer produced an article of most beautiful quality. The manufacture of crape for dresses, and of embroidered crape and damask shawls resembling those of China, was introduced here about the year 1823, and carried on to a very considerable extent, affording lucrative employment to numbers of females, whose ingenuity and skill have produced specimens in many instances equal to those imported from Canton: this manufacture is still pursued, though less extensively than formerly. The shawls at present chiefly made are of three kinds; either entirely of silk, a mixture of silk and cotton, or wholly of cotton. The trade in them has been rapidly increasing, and the value of the quantities produced in a late year was estimated at nearly £1,000,000. The chenille shawl was introduced into the town by Mr. Buchanan, afterwards of Glasgow, and is made on a very extensive scale: these shawls, of velvet on silk, from their extreme softness and the variety of their colours are in great estimation. The *thread* manufacture, in which cotton has been recently used in the place of linen, affords employment to many persons, and the quantity annually made is estimated at £100,000. The total number of *looms* in the town is more than 6,000. Machinery of every kind, and on the most improved principles, is used in all the factories; and for facilitating the operations, and bringing to greater perfection the articles made, numerous ingenious contrivances have been suggested, and successfully applied, both by the masters and the workmen.

The printing of silks and muslins is carried on to a limited extent, and the weaving of tartan employs numerous persons. The cotton manufacture, which was first attempted at Dovecothall, is also pursued, and on a considerable scale: there are at present three factories in the town, two of which are very extensive. An iron foundry on a large scale has been established for more than fifty years; and connected with it are works for the manufacture of steam engines and all kinds of machinery. There are also a manufactory for gasometers, and iron boats for canal navigation; three large brass foundries in the town. A very extensive tannery is conducted with great success, There are three public breweries, two of which are extensive; three distilleries; a large soap manufactory; and seven bleach fields, to most of which capacious reservoirs have been attached by the company for supplying Paisley with water. Two banks have been established in the town, in which are also three branch banks connected with Edinburgh and Glasgow, and numerous offices for fire and life insurance: the post office has several deliveries daily; and the revenue, before the adoption of the system of the penny postage, amounted to £3,194. The market, which is amply supplied, is weekly, on Thursday; and there are four annual fairs, for three days each, respectively commencing the third Thursday in February, the third Thursday in May, the third Thursday in August, and the second Thursday in November. At the August fair, the Paisley races, which have been long established, attract a numerous assemblage of visitors.

The Glasgow, Paisley & Johnstone Canal, for which an act of parliament was obtained in 1805 was commenced in 1807 and the Paisley to Johnstone stretch was finished in 1810. In the following year, the portion between this town and Glasgow was opened. The whole navigation is eleven miles in length, about twenty-eight feet in width, and four feet and a half average depth; and was completed at an expense of £130,000. In addition to the boats for goods and merchandise, three boats were at first handsomely fitted up for passengers, each capable of carrying one hundred persons. The passage was performed in less than an hour; the number of passengers annually conveyed was 423,186, and the amount of fares received by the proprietors more than £9,000. Not less than sixty-four horses were employed for these boats. By a recent arrangement, however, with railway companies, the conveyance of passengers is to be discontinued for twenty-one years, and the traffic confined to heavy goods, of which 68,063 tons were carried in the year ending 30th September 1844. The railway from Paisley to Renfrew was constructed by a company under an act obtained in 1835; and the line was opened in May 1837. The amount of capital is £23,000. The Glasgow, Paisley & Greenock railway was commenced under an act passed in 1837; The portion between Glasgow and Paisley was opened on 14th July 1840: the capital of the company is £866,666.The Glasgow, Paisley, Kilmarnock & Ayr Railway proceeds through Paisley on a viaduct, resting on several arches of different spans, according to the width of the streets and roads passed over, of which there are seven. The works of this railway were commenced in May 1838; and the whole line, forty miles between Glasgow and Ayr was opened in August 1840.

APPENDIX II

Page numbers in bold refer to Fowler's Directory page numbers.

Note on the census of 1841

The 1841 census was taken on Sunday 6 June under provisions in the Census Act 1840 (3 and 4 Vict. c.99) and Census Amendment Act (4 and 5 Vict. c.7) and in Scotland enumeration duties were carried out by the official schoolmaster in each parish and the sheriff deputes (for counties and stewartries) and provosts (for burghs).

Because there was inevitably some resistance in giving information, penalties had to be introduced 'for refusing Information, or giving false Answers'.

Special care must be taken in interpreting the census results relates to the ages given. The enumerators' instructions were to round down ages, though in many instances they clearly have given the proper age.

There are the usual difficulties of differing spellings, uncertainty of age and variation in the house identification numbers. Some streets were re-numbered at this time as a result of the introduction of the organised postal system and the introduction of the Penny Post in 1840. Street numbering in the early nineteenth century was somewhat haphazard, since with a small population most people knew where others lived. The introduction of the Penny Post meant that individual properties had to be clearly identified and, during the course of the century the Paisley house numbering system was altered at least once. This means, that where we record differing house numbers, they may be, in many cases, describing the same property. Added to this is the fact that the Directory and the Census are recording a mobile population, so changes occur between April 1841 and the census, the preparation of the Directory and the notes added at the beginning of 1842.

Page 13
[1] 1829 and 1835 Directories: Blacksmiths, Lylesland; 1841 Census: James aged 50 and John aged 55
[2] 1829 Directory: John & Son, bleachers
[3] 1838 Directory: Manufacturer, 3 Cumberland Court, 110 Causeyside
[4] 1841 Census: Bowling Green house
[5] 1841 Census: living at 85 Canal street

Page 14
[1] 1841 Census: with wife Mary aged 45
[2] 1829 Directory: 104 High street, house 103 High street; Ordinary Director, Paisley Commercial Banking Company, 4 Smithhills
[3] 1841 Census: teacher, 9 Castle street

Page 15
[1] Convener and Secretary, Firemen Committee; Treasurer Scotch Thistle Friendly Society (est. 1812), 52 Broomlands; Curator Paisley Library
[2] Preses Mortcloth Society (est. 1820), 65 Broomlands; Secretary Equitable Society (est. 1825), 69 High street
[3] 1835 Directory: Armour, Robert & Co., provision stores, 216 High street
[4] Director of Town Hospital, 7 New Sneddon; clerk to Albion Friendly Society (est. 1815), 8 George street

Page 16
[1] Stent Master for the Burgh; Director of Town Hospital, 7 New Sneddon; President Equitable Society (est. 1825)
[2] Public works representative for Foxbar Sabbath and Weekday evening schools
[3] Clerk to Ayrshire Society (est. 1773), 72 Love street
[4] Treasurer Bakers' Society (est. 1777); monument in Woodside Cemetery: died 22/2/1884 aged 81 and his wife Janet Buchan died 6/2/1883 aged 71
[5] Box-master Hammermen's Society (est. 1760)
[6] Commissioner of Police 7th Ward; Preses Ayrshire Society (est. 1773)
[7] Congregational representative Sabbath and Weekday evening schools

Page 17
[1] Stent Master for the Burgh
[2] cotton dyer; Representative for west division Sabbath and Weekday evening schools
[3] Preses 1st section Young Friendly Society (est. 1802); 1841 Census: and son James, aged 20, Caledonia street
[4] Stent Master for the Burgh; monument in Thread Street UP Churchyard: Property of William Barbour, cabinetmaker, and Janet Boyle his wife
[5] Monument in Woodside Cemetery: of Canal Bank 17/9/1808 – 5/3/1895
[6] Manager qualified by subscription of the Dispensary and House of Recovery, 11 Bridge street; President Paisley Female Benevolent Society (est. 1811)
[7] Deacon Shoemaker's Society (est. 1701) 29 High street
[8] Bailie; Director Hutcheson's Charity School, Orr street

Page 18
[1] 1829 Directory: warper. Dyer's wynd
[2] In 1837 built first steam engine for Mr. Galloway's works. 1835 Directory: Galloway and Walker, shawl warehouse men, 115 Causeyside and 18 Friday street, London
[3] 1835 Directory: Barr's Paisley Apothecaries' Hall
[4] 1829 Directory: at Buck's Head Tea rooms, 232 High street
[5] Curator and President Paisley Library
[6] Manager qualified by subscription of the Dispensary and House of Recovery, 11 Bridge street
[7] 1841 Census: with wife Janet also 25 and two small children Jessie,2, and Hugh, 7 months
[8] 1829 Directory: flesher and spirit dealer (stabling), 1 West Broomlands street

Page 19
[1] 1829 Directory: Manufacturer, 11 Barclay street
[2] Dick & McGregor Directory 1840: house, 12 Wellmeadow street

Page 20
[1] Town Councillor; 1841 Census: wife Agnes aged 30 grocer; Dick & McGregor Directory 1840: provision merchant, 18 Causeyside; shops 95 Broomlands and 1 Bridge street; monument in Thread Street UP Churchyard: died 1842
[2] Senior key keeper St. Mirren's Lodge (No.128) (est. 1749); monument in Woodside Cemetery: died 25/7/1858 aged 52
[3] Manager elected by subscribers of the Dispensary and House of Recovery, 11 Bridge street; Protestant Director Roman Catholic school, Orr street; Dick & McGregor Directory 1840: shawl manufacturer;
[4] 1841 Census: William, aged 50

Page 21

[1] Manager qualified by subscription of the Dispensary and House of Recovery, 11 Bridge street and Manager elected by subscribers of the Dispensary and House of Recovery, 11 Bridge street; Secretary and Treasurer Roman Catholic school, Orr street

[2] Protestant Director Roman Catholic School, Orr street; Director Infant school, 12 Lawn street; Paisley Total Abstinence Society (est. 1836)

[3] 1829 Directory: haberdasher, 269 High street; In 1837 bought 20 shares in the Glasgow, Paisley, Kilmarnock & Ayr Railway for £1,000

[4] Chairman National Security Savings Bank, 4 Christie Terrace; Manager qualified by subscription of the Dispensary and House of Recovery, 11 Bridge street; Curator Paisley Library; Curator and Treasurer Theological Library, 22 Moss street; Director Deaf and Dumb Institution; Ordinary Director Paisley Gas Light Company (est. 1823); governor, Paisley Water Company (est. 1834; 1829 Directory: haberdasher, 231 High street house, 9 Bridge street; in 1837 bought 40 shares in the Glasgow, Paisley, Kilmarnock & Ayr Railway for £2,000

[5] Manager qualified by subscription of the Dispensary and House of Recovery, 11 Bridge street; Director Deaf and Dumb Institution; monument Abbey Churchyard: Andrew died 17/9/1856 aged 69, his wife Eliza Stewart died 19/3/1871 aged 80

[6] Dick & McGregor Directory 1840: shawl manufacturers

[7] permit writer; Permit Officer, Excise and Permit Office, Christie's Buildings, 109 High street

[8] Town Councillor; Director and convener of Town Hospital, 7 New Sneddon; Curator and Treasurer Paisley Library; monument in Woodside Cemetery: M.D., died 23/12/1846 aged 36

Page 22

[1] 1835 Directory: Andrew, merchant

[2] 1835 Directory: John, baker

[3] commenced 1840

[4] Dick & McGregor Directory 1840: muslin manufacturer, 10 Wardrop street

[5] Monument in Woodside Cemetery: died 2/3/1855

[6] Low parish Paisley (Burgh) Road Director (est. 1834)

Page 23

[1] 1829 Directory: cloth and spirit merchant, 59 High street

[2] 1841 Census: flesh stand, 2 School wynd

[3] Chairman, Scottish Amicable Life Assurance and Endowment Society; Director for St. George's church Hutcheson's Charity School, Orr street; Director Infant school, 12 Lawn street; Director Deaf and Dumb Institution; In 1837 bought 10 shares in the Glasgow, Paisley, Kilmarnock & Ayr Railway for £500

[4] Congregational representative Sabbath and Weekday evening schools

[5] Paisley Total Abstinence Society (est. 1836); 1838 built Teetotal Tower at Sandyford, opened 1840. John Urie, *Reminiscences of Eighty Years*, Paisley, Gardner, 1908, p.33: 'The wife of Geordie Caldwell, a printer in Paisley, was also a bit of a character. She kept the Teetotal Tower, a building between Paisley and Renfrew. There she served out lemonade and ginger beer to the young lads who frequented her place. I remember her well as she dispensed her hospitality attired in a silk dress, with the heads of stockings drawn up over her arms as sleeves. The attractions of the place were greatly enhanced by a camera obscura, to which admission was gained on payment of a penny. You got a fine view of the surrounding country in that darkened room.'

[6] James Caldwell the writer was Clerk of Supply and County Clerk, Renfrewshire 1850-1909; Clerk to Master Tailors' Society (established 1658); Clerk to Wrights' Society (est. 1723); Clerk to Widow and Orphan Society (est. 1776); 1841 Census: 95 High street; monument in Woodside Cemetery: writer, Craigielea Place, born 12/2/1818 died 21/6/1909

Page 24

[1] Preses Journeymen Tailors' Benevolent Funeral Society (est. 1835); 1829 Directory: and habitmakers, 234 High street; 1841 Census: aged 70, 49 Storie street

[2] Ordinary Director, Paisley Commercial Banking Company, 4 Smithhills and Scottish Amicable Life Assurance and Endowment Society; Manager elected by subscribers of the Dispensary and House of Recovery, 11 Bridge street; Protestant Director Roman Catholic school, Orr street

[3] 1841 Census: 24 Oakshaw street

[4] Treasurer, New Town Road Committee (est. 1792)

[5] Low parish convener Paisley (Burgh) Road Director (est. 1834); 1841 Census: Robert aged 15 spirit dealer

[6] Manager qualified by subscription of the Dispensary and House of Recovery, 11 Bridge street

[7] Preses Master Tailors' Society (established 1658)

Page 25

[1] 1841 Census: both aged 35, cotton dyer and Duncan, aged 30, silk dyer

[2] 1841 Census: John Gilmour aged 20 at 24 Orchard street

[3] 1829 Directory: Thread manufacturer, house 79 New Sneddon Manager qualified by subscription of the Dispensary and House of Recovery, 11 Bridge street; Director and Treasurer Hutcheson's Charity School, Orr street

[4] Commenced business 1812 – closed 1852

Page 26

[1] Manager elected by subscribers of the Dispensary and House of Recovery, 11 Bridge street

[2] Dick & McGregor Directory 1840: silk gauze manufacturers

[3] 1835 Directory: John F Carswell & Co., merchants; Dick & McGregor Directory 1840: shawl merchants
[4] Commissioner of Police 4th Ward
[5] 1835 Directory: chandler 57 Canal street
[6] 1841 Census: High street
[7] Commenced business 1835 – closed 1886
[8] John Clapperton was a non-conformist minister in Johnstone, Renfrewshire, in the 1840s.
[9] Director Deaf and Dumb Institution 1829 Directory: thread manufacturer, house Seedhill; monument in Abbey Churchyard: died 19/10/1865 aged 82 and his wife Agnes McFarlane died 11/9/1836 aged 26 erected by James and Robert Clark for their father

Page 27
[1] Coats and Clarke merged on 1st July 1896. The merger was discussed over lunch in the Western Club, Glasgow and was overheard by John Augustus Holms, stockbroker, who immediately bought up shares before the public announcement and made a fortune, which led to him being a collector of the stature of William Burrell
[2] Dick & McGregor Directory 1840: Mrs. R, late Paton, scotch cloth merchant, 103 Cross, house, 101 High street
[3] Commenced business 1832. See note 2 above
[4] Commissioner of Police 6th Ward; Treasurer Grocers' Company (est. 1824); High parish Paisley (Burgh) Road Director (est. 1834)
[5] 1829 Directory: 7 Calside
[6] 1829 Directory: Thomas, druggist 41 Wellmeadow street and 1835 Directory

Page 28
[1] Independent 1829 Directory: merchant, 5 Garthland place; 1835 Directory: merchant, 110 Causeyside house, 22 St. James' street
[2] President Priors' Croft Bowling Green (est. 1840), 50 Storie street; Director Paisley Coffee Room, 107 High street
[3] Dick & McGregor Directory 1840: Thurscraig; 1841 Census: James aged 60 bleacher and Margaret aged 60 bleacher 12 Bridge street

Page 29
[1] Dick & McGregor Directory 1840: shawl manufacturer
[2] Stent Master; Collector for Corporation of Merchants (est. 1725)
[3] 1829 Directory: William flesher and vintner and horse setter 18 New street; 1835 Directory: 37 Causeyside
[4] Monument in Woodside Cemetery: died 9/4/1852

Page 30
[1] 1829 Directory: manufacturer, 2 Gauze street Preses Paisley Friendly Society (est. 1783); Preses Paisley Croft Society (est. 1761), Abbey street
[2] 1829 Directory: Andrew, machine maker 20 New Smithhills, house 18 Gauze street; Dick & McGregor Directory 1840: shawl manufacturers

[3] 1829 Directory: teacher of dancing, academy, 25 School wynd, house 82 High street
[4] Secretary and Agent, Scottish Amicable Life Assurance and Endowment Society; in 1837 bought 30 shares in the Glasgow, Paisley, Kilmarnock & Ayr Railway for £500
[5] 1829 Directory: John, vintner, 1 St. Mirren street
[6] Curator and President the Trades' Library 42 New street
[7] 1841 Census: Orr street

Page 31
[1] agricultural labourer 32 Castle street
[2] Ordinary Director Paisley Gas Light Company (est. 1823)
[3] Dick & McGregor Directory 1840: shawl manufacturer; monument in Oakshaw East: late manufacturer, died 13/7/1847 aged 34
[4] 1829 Directory: Adam, grocer and spirit dealer, 10 Back Sneddon; monument in Thread Street UP Churchyard: Janet Baxter wife of Adam Currie

Page 32
[1] Treasurer Hope Friendly Society (est. 1812) 122 George street
[2] Dick & McGregor Directory 1840: muslin manufacturer, 2 Gauze street, house 29 Thread street
[3] Director Paisley Coffee Room, 107 High street; Treasurer Society for Reformation of Manners (est. 1757), 20 Orchard street
[4] Collector for Ayrshire Society (est. 1773); clerk to Rose Friendly Society (est. 1812), 95 Causeyside
[5] Preses Society for Reformation of Manners (est. 1757); Ordinary Director Paisley Water Company (est. 1834); 1829 Directory: tobacconist and candlemaker, 25 High street, house 29 High street; monument in Woodside Cemetery: died 28/10/1856 aged 72

Page 33
[1] Collector for Shoemakers' Society (est. 1701)
[2] 1841 Census: 70 Canal street
[3] 1835 Directory: 'Lady' Downie, 9 Orr square
[4] Director, Scottish Amicable Life Assurance and Endowment Society; Preses Widow and Orphan Society (est. 1776)
[5] President Sabbath and Weekday evening schools
[6] Preses Hope Friendly Society (est. 1812)
[7] Commissioner of Police 8th Ward
[8] 1841 Census: born 1821
[9] 1841 Census: born 1781

Page 34
[1] Curator Theological Library, 22 Moss street
[2] clerk to Grocers' Company (est. 1824)
[3] 1829 Directory: starcher and silk boiler, 70 Causeyside

[4] 1829 Directory: at No.7; 1835 Directory: John, spirit dealer, 6 New Sneddon

Page 35

[1] 1841 Census: 33 George street, Falconer, James, aged 40 licensed pawnbroker; 1841 Census: and wife Marion

[2] merchant; Clerk to Paisley United Curling Club (est. 1829)

[3] 1841 Census: with wife Jane aged 36

[4] Thread Manufacturer commenced business 1837 – closed 1860; Director Paisley Coffee Room, 107 High street; Protestant Director Roman Catholic school, Orr street; Ordinary Director Paisley Gas Light Company (est. 1823); Extraordinary Director Paisley Water Company (est. 1834); Extraordinary Director, Paisley Commercial Banking Company, 4 Smithills and Director, Scottish Amicable Life Assurance and Endowment Society; monument in Abbey Churchyard: of Allargue and Breda, died 14/2/1863 aged 81, his wife Jean Nairn died 14/4/1870, both interred in Strathdon Church

[5] 1829 Directory: Patrick, grocer and chandler, 221 High street 1841 Census: Catherine, tallow chandler

[6] Director Paisley Coffee Room, 107 High street; Director Deaf and Dumb Institution

Page 36

[1] 1841 Census: Finlayson, William, aged 40, florist, Seedhill, wife Catherine aged 35, seedsman

[2] Middle parish Paisley (Burgh) Road Director (est. 1834)

[3] Serjeant fireman; Senior Warden St. Mirren's Lodge (No.128) (est. 1749); Dick & McGregor Directory 1840: fireman, No.1 Red engine

[4] Monument in Woodside Cemetery: his relict Bethia Jaap died 3/3/1872 aged 78; Stent Master for the Burgh

[5] 1841 Census: with wife Mary aged 30, 53 High street. The accident took place in 1834; the victims were Andrew Fleming, corkcutter and pawnbroker, and his wife, Elizabeth Ewing. The house (Silverae, 43 Irvine Road, Largs) was demolished in 1987

[6] 1829 Directory: vintner, 19 Old Smithhills

[7] Dick & McGregor Directory 1840: shawl manufacturers

[8] 1829 Directory: manufacturer, 169 Causeyside Manager qualified by subscription of the Dispensary and House of Recovery, 11 Bridge street

[9] Low parish Paisley (Burgh) Road Director (est. 1834); 1829 Directory: Foulds & Co., brass founders 60 High street; Matthew Foulds, cooper, 228 High street

Page 37

[1] Ordinary Director Paisley Gas Light Company (est. 1823); Ordinary Director Paisley Water Company (est. 1834)

[2] Commissioner of Police 1st Ward

Appendix II

[3] Manager qualified by subscription of the Dispensary and House of Recovery, 11 Bridge street
[4] Manager elected by subscribers of the Dispensary and House of Recovery, 11 Bridge street
[5] 1829 Directory: James Futt, grocer, 15 Ferguslie; 1835 Directory: James, grocer, 105 George street

Page 38
[1] Manager elected by subscribers of the Dispensary and House of Recovery, 11 Bridge street; Director Paisley Coffee Room, 107 High street; Secretary Deaf and Dumb Institution; monument in Woodside Cemetery: 2/2/1805 – 17/1/1877
[2] 1829 Directory: manufacturer, 3 Silk street
[3] 1841 Census: 90 Canal street
[4] In 1837 bought 10 shares in the Glasgow, Paisley, Kilmarnock & Ayr Railway for £500
[5] 1841 Census: Mrs Andrew, glove and hosiery shop Christie terrace

Page 39
[1] Middle parish Paisley (Burgh) Road Director (est. 1834)
[2] Treasurer and Secretary Director Paisley Coffee Room, 107 High street; Clerk for Shoemakers' Society (est. 1701); Clerk for Maltmen's Society (ext.1703); Clerk for Corporation of Merchants (est. 1725); Clerk for Hammermen's Society (est. 1760) 1841 Census: and Robert aged 22
[3] Took as an apprentice James Robertson, born 1832, who later opened his own shop at 86 Causeyside in 1859 where marmalade was made. He died in 1914
[4] 1829 Directory: canal Treasurer; Manager elected by subscribers of the Dispensary and House of Recovery, 11 Bridge street; Director Paisley Coffee Room, 107 High street

Page 40
[1] Preses Rose Friendly Society (est. 1812)
[2] Stent Master for the Burgh
[3] 1829 Directory: Andrew spirit dealer 13 High street
[4] Disburser 1st section Young Friendly Society (est. 1802)
[5] Director, Scottish Amicable Life Assurance and Endowment Society; Manager elected by subscribers of the Dispensary and House of Recovery, 11 Bridge street; Protestant Director Roman Catholic school, Orr street
[6] 1841 Census: Janet aged 25 or Helen, dressmaker aged 15 or Isabella aged 15

Page 41
[1] Commenced business 1833 – closed 1849

Page 42
[1] Dick & McGregor Directory 1840: shawl manufacturer
[2] 1841 Census: and son aged 20

³ Stent Master for the Burgh; 1829 Directory: John & Co., muslin and shawl manufacturers, 172 Causeyside, house 110 Causeyside;
⁴ Dick & McGregor Directory 1840: shawl warehouse 7 St. Mirren street
⁵ Ordinary Director, Paisley Commercial Banking Company, 4 Smithhills; Extraordinary director Paisley & Renfrew Railway (est. 1837)
⁶ Senior standard bearer St. Mirren's Lodge (No.128) (est. 1749); 1829 Directory: Mason, 7 Sir Michael street

Page 43
¹ Captain Archers' Society (est. 1806)
² Public works representative for Lounsdale Sabbath and Weekday evening schools
³ 1829 Directory: jeweller, 49 High street

Page 44
¹ Clerk to Old Weavers' Society (est. 1702)
² Preses 4th section Young Friendly Society (est. 1802)

Page 45
¹ Director of Town Hospital, 7 New Sneddon; President St. Andrew's Sickness Assurance Society (est. 1828); Treasurer Equitable Society (est. 1825); 1829 Directory: and spindle and fly manufacturer, 151 and 152 High street
² 1829 Directory: druggist, 39 Broomlands; 1835 Directory: Hendry, R and O, 15 Broomlands
³ Ordinary Director Paisley Gas Light Company (est. 1823)
⁴ Deputy governor Paisley Water Company (est. 1834)
⁵ Cashier, National Security Savings Bank
⁶ 1841 Census: James aged 25 and Thomas aged 25 tobacco shopmen
⁷ Commissioner of Police for the New Town; 1829 Directory: senior, teller in Union Bank, house 4 East Buchanan street
⁸ Manager qualified by subscription of the Dispensary and House of Recovery, 11 Bridge street; Ordinary director Paisley Water Company (est. 1834); father of the great collector, John Augustus Holms of Formakin

Page 46
¹ Manager elected by subscribers of the Dispensary and House of Recovery, 11 Bridge street; Director Deaf and Dumb Institution; monument in Woodside Cemetery: manufacturer died 29/1/ ? drowned in crossing Holy Loch 2/4/1853 ?
² Treasurer Wrights' Society (est. 1723); Preses 3rd section Young Friendly Society (est. 1802)

Page 47
¹ Director of Town Hospital, 7 New Sneddon
² 1841 Census: 30 Old Sneddon
³ Preses Paisley United Curling Club (est. 1829)
⁴ Commissioner of Police 2nd Ward; Stent Master for the Burgh

Appendix II

Page 48
[1] 1841 Census: 12 St. Mirren street
[2] Disburser 2nd section Young Friendly Society (est. 1802)
[3] Treasurer Paisley Total Abstinence Society (est. 1836) 1841 Census: Thomas Jaap, aged 30, shoemaker, 94 High street
[4] 1841 Census: and John aged 20, grocer and spirit dealer, 52 Storie street west side
[5] Ordinary Director Paisley Gas Light Company (est. 1823)
[6] statutory clerk and law agent Paisley Gas Light Company (est. 1823)
[7] Commenced business 1832 – closed 1859
[8] 1841 Census: James Jeffrey
[9] Monument in Thread Street UP Churchyard: died 18/1/1845 and his wife Wilhelmina Bushey died 29/12/1868 aged 82

Page 49
[1] Curator Paisley Library
[2] 1841 Census: 66 Canal street
[3] Director of Town Hospital, 7 New Sneddon; monument in Woodside Cemetery

Page 50
[1] Revd., President Paisley Total Abstinence Society (est. 1836)
[2] Memorial in Woodside Cemetery
[3] Dick & McGregor Directory 1840: muslin manufacturers
[4] Monument in Woodside Cemetery, died 12/12/1852 aged 70
[5] Commenced business 1823 – closed 1863
[6] Roman Catholic Director Roman Catholic school, Orr street Thread Manufacturer commenced business 1812 – closed 1906
[7] Thread Manufacturer commenced business 1833 – closed 1845

Page 51
[1] A shawl-printer
[2] Town Councillor and Councillor, Firemen Committee; Manager elected by subscribers of the Dispensary and House of Recovery, 11 Bridge street; Director of Town Hospital, 7 New Sneddon

Page 52
[1] publican
[2] 1841 Census: John aged 65 joiner, in the house Robert aged 30 no occupation
[3] Secretary Paisley Young Men's Sabbath Morning Association (est. 1833), 10 St. Mirren street
[4] Dick & McGregor Directory 1840: Robert Laird house 10 Gauze street
[5] Commissioner of Police 7th Ward; Stent Master for the Burgh
[6] 1829 Directory: dyer, 38 Moss street

Page 53
[1] Director Paisley Coffee Room 107 High street

[2] 1829 Directory: merchant; Director Paisley Coffee Room 107 High street
[3] 1841 Census: Lochwinnoch

Page 54
[1] Extraordinary Director Paisley Gas Light Company (est. 1823)
[2] 1829 Directory: John, 59 Wellmeadow; 1841 Census: John aged 50, John aged 20 and James aged 18 turners; monument in Woodside Cemetery: wood turner died 29/6/1880
[3] 1835 Directory: grocer and spirit dealer; Dick & McGregor Directory 1840: bleacher, general washing field, Espedair, head of Causeyside
[4] Extraordinary Director Paisley Gas Light Company (est. 1823)
[5] Deacon Bakers' Society (est. 1777)
[6] 1829 Directory: London Genuine Tea Co., 6 Old Smithhills
[7] Extraordinary Director Paisley Gas Light Company (est. 1823)

Page 55
[1] Monument in Thread Street UP Churchyard: died 22/8/1843 aged 60 wife Mary Crawford died 15/3/1842 aged 59
[2] 1841 Census: New street with father John
[3] 1829 Directory: Manson & Faulds, reedmakers
[4] 1841 Census: and Alexander, aged 25

Page 56
[1] 1829 and 1835 Directory: manufacturers, 22 Causeyside, house 7 West Croft street
[2] Secretary Renfrewshire Agricultural Society (est. 1819); Extraordinary Director Paisley Gas Light Company (est. 1823); clerk to Paisley Water Company (est. 1834); Director Paisley Coffee Room ,107 High street; 1841 Census: 1 Love street; monument in Woodside Cemetery: 4/9/1804 – 1/12/1860; in 1837 bought 2 shares in the Glasgow, Paisley, Kilmarnock & Ayr Railway for £100
[3] Ann, 1829 Directory: Mrs. Andrew, grocer and vintner, 20 Old Sneddon; 1841 Census: victualler Old Sneddon, Shoemaker's Lane

Page 57
[1] 1841 Census: William, aged 25, painter and paperhanger, 41 High street
[2] Director of Town Hospital, 7 New Sneddon; Secretary Young Friendly Society (est. 1802)
[3] Manager elected by subscribers of the Dispensary and House of Recovery, 11 Bridge street
[4] 1841 Census: with son John aged 25

Page 58
[1] Dick & McGregor Directory 1840: shawl manufacturer, 12 Wardrop street, house 24 Ferguslie

Appendix II

² Monument in Thread Street UP Churchyard: merchant, Glasgow formerly Shawl Manufacturer died 22/6/1873 aged 83 his wife Janet Gibson died 3/3/1881 aged 83
³ Treasurer Paisley Philharmonic Society (est. 1834)
⁴ Treasurer St. Mirren's Lodge (No.128) (est. 1749) 1829 Directory: Mills & Faulds, masons, 35 Calside
⁵ 1841 Census: with wife Agnes aged 40

Page 59
¹ 1835 Directory: manufacturer, 6 Brown's lane, house 40 High street

Page 60
¹ Clerk to Fleshers' Society (est. 1751)
² Librarian Paisley Library
³ 1841 Census: Underwood road
⁴ Extraordinary Director Paisley Gas Light Company (est. 1823)
⁵ 1841 Census: 7 Marshall lane
⁶ 1841 Census: and Armstrong Munn aged 20, merchants, Storie street

Page 61
¹ Bailie; Director Hutcheson's Charity School, Orr street
² Director Deaf and Dumb Institution
³ Monument in Woodside Cemetery: 3/7/1797 – 4/7/1859
⁴ Stent Master for the Burgh
⁵ Monument in Woodside Cemetery: Manufacturer died 5/6/1865
⁶ Director Deaf and Dumb Institution

Page 62
¹ 1829 Directory: shawl manufacturer, 150 Causeyside, house 13 Barclay street; Dick & McGregor Directory 1840: shawl warehouse
² 1829 Directory: Alexander & Son, 31 High street

Page 62
¹ Dick & McGregor Directory 1840: muslin manufacturers 14 St. Mirren street
² 1829 Directory: manufacturer
³ 1829 Directory: clerk Saucel Brewery, house 15 Saucel
⁴ Roman Catholic Director Roman Catholic school, Orr street; Secretary and Treasurer Medical Society (est. 1818)

Page 63
¹ Monument in Thread Street UP Churchyard: died November 1849 aged 94 and wife Janet Harvey died February 1820 aged 53
² Preses Roman Catholic School, Orr street; Director Deaf and Dumb Institution; Dick & McGregor Directory 1840: shawl manufacturers
³ Director and convener Paisley Coffee Room, 107 High street; Convener of Merchants' society; Director Hutcheson's Charity School, Orr street; Box-master Maltmen's Society (est. 1703); Convener Corporation of Merchants (est. 1725)
⁴ Secretary Sabbath and Weekday evening schools

Page 64
[1] Commissioner of Police 8th Ward
[2] 1829 Directory: Duncan & Co., dyers, 4 Smithhills

Page 65
[1] Treasurer, Primitive Methodist Sabbath morning and evening school, 10 Abbey close
[2] 1841 Census: and David aged 35 at 38 Moss street

Page 67
[1] Dick & McGregor Directory 1840: shawl manufacturers
[2] Medical department of the Dispensary and House of Recovery, 11 Bridge street; President Medical Society (est. 1818)
[3] Curator Theological Library, 22 Moss street; Congregational representative Sabbath and Weekday evening schools

Page 68
[1] 1829 Directory: David, senior, spirit dealer and warper, 16 Causeyside
[2] 1829 and 1835 Directory: Patrick, grocer and grain merchant; 1841 Census: Jean
[3] President Infant school 12 Lawn street; President Deaf and Dumb Institution

Page 69
[1] Director for High church Hutcheson's Charity School, Orr street; Director Infant school, 12 Lawn street
[2] 1841 Census: 1 Maxwell street
[3] Dick & McGregor Directory 1840: Alexander, shawl manufacturer

Page 70
[1] 1841 Census: wright, 5 Wellmeadow
[2] Dick & McGregor Directory 1840: shawl manufacturer; Stent Master for the Burgh
[3] Congregational representative Sabbath and Weekday evening schools
[4] 1829 Directory: William, cowfeeder, 132 Causeyside; 1835 Directory: Mrs.William

Page 71
[1] Commissioner of Police 1st Ward; Director of Town Hospital, 7 New Sneddon; Roman Catholic Director Roman Catholic school, Orr street; Junior visitor of trades St. Mirren's Lodge (No.128) (est. 1749); Preses Catholic Friendly Society (est. 1817); Middle parish Paisley (Burgh) Road Director (est. 1834)
[2] Manager qualified by subscription of the Dispensary and House of Recovery, 11 Bridge street; 1841 Census: with son John aged 18
[3] Extraordinary Director, Paisley Commercial Banking Company, 4 Smithhills; Right Worshipful Master. St. Mirren's Lodge (No.128) (est. 1749)
[4] 1835 Directory: manufacturer, 6 Causeyside

[5] 1829 Directory: James, manufacturer, 12 Gauze street; Dick & McGregor Directory 1840: shawl manufacturer
[6] 1841 Census: living in New street

Page 72

[1] 1841 Census: Stevenson street
[2] Deacon Fleshers' Society (est. 1751)
[3] Medical department of the Dispensary and House of Recovery, 11 Bridge street; Director of Town Hospital, 7 New Sneddon
[4] Commissioner of Police 3rd Ward; 1841 Census: 45 Oakshaw street married to Mrs. Paton, linen draper, below
[5] Commissioner of Police 4th Ward
[6] 1835 Directory: Mrs. William, scotch cloth merchant, 103 High street, house 4 Moss street; 1841 Census: 45 Oakshaw street
[7] Town Councillor, Commissioner of Police 2nd Ward; Collector Widow and Orphan Society (est. 1776)
[8] Dick & McGregor Directory 1840: Patrick, Elliot & Burns, shawl manufacturers, 112 Causeyside
[9] Ordinary Director Paisley & Renfrew Railway (est. 1837); monument in Woodside Cemetery: baker and miller died 14/11/1852 aged 56

Page 73

[1] Treasurer, Firemen Committee; monument in Oakshaw East: erected by William Philips, merchant, for his father Robert, died 25/11/1830 aged 74
[2] 1841 Census: independent, 1 Muslin street
[3] 1841 Census: Muslin street
[4] Manager qualified by subscription of the Dispensary and House of Recovery, 11 Bridge street; Deputy governor Paisley & Renfrew Railway (est. 1837); in 1837 bought 6 shares in the Glasgow, Paisley, Kilmarnock & Ayr Railway for £300

Page 74

[1] Monument in Woodside Cemetery: hermetically sealed metal vault – born 1816, died 1876
[2] Dick & McGregor Directory 1840: shawl manufacturers
[3] 1841 Census: shawl manufacturer 29 Glen street SG 58/42/17 – retired to Gourock, died 6/3/1849; Alexander Borland, accountant in Glasgow, Robert Hendry sometime druggist in Paisley, now in Helensburgh, and William Wilson, manufacturer in Paisley, trustees; 1841 Census: aged 45 shawl manufacturer. His brother, John c.1795-1858, settled in Canada in 1821 in North Sherbroule township, married Elizabeth Macdonald 1793-1847, granted ownership 28/11/1839 and then moved to Perth, Canada. Returned to Paisley and married Janet (Sarah) Glen in September 1848
[4] Dick & McGregor Directory 1840: shawl manufacturers
[5] 1829 Directory: 107 Causeyside

Page 75
[1] Preses 2nd section Young Friendly Society (est. 1802)
[2] 1829 Directory: blacksmiths and bell hangers 4 Orr street
[3] 1841 Census: William Reid aged 35 living at Seedhill with mother
[4] 1841 Census: James Reid aged 35, dyer, Seedhill
[5] 1835 Directory: grocer and grain dealer

Page 76
[1] 1829 Directory: James, baker and spirit dealer, 79 Storie street
[2] Ordinary Director, Paisley Commercial Banking Company, 4 Smithhills; Manager elected by subscribers of the Dispensary and House of Recovery, 11 Bridge street and Treasurer; Ordinary Director Paisley Water Company (est. 1834); Ordinary Director Paisley & Renfrew Railway (est. 1837)
[3] Bailie; Director Hutcheson's Charity School, Orr street
[4] President New Town Road Committee (est. 1792)
[5] Dick & McGregor Directory 1840: shawl manufacturers, house 37 Canal street

Page 77
[1] shawl manufacturer
[2] 1829 and 1835 Directory: William, hat manufacturer, 242 High street, house 243 High street
[3] 1841 Census: Barclay street

Page 78
[1] Commenced business 1827 – closed 1896
[2] 1841 Census: Barclay street
[3] Dick & McGregor Directory 1840: shawl manufacturers
[4] 1835 Directory: silk and shawl warehouse, 31 Gauze street

Page 79
[1] Treasurer, National Security Savings Bank; Treasurer Deaf and Dumb Institution; Ordinary Director Paisley Gas Light Company (est. 1823); monument in Woodside Cemetery: died 2/4/1856 aged 69
[2] Dick & McGregor Directory 1840: shawl manufacturer
[3] 1829 Directory: Samuel Shannon, clothlapper, 162 Causeyside; 1835 Directory: & Son; 1841 Census: aged 45 clothlapper

Page 80

Page 81
[1] 1841 Census: living at 107 Causeyside
[2] Town Councillor; Manager New Town Road Committee (est. 1792)

Page 82
[1] Preses Reform Registration Association (est. 1832); Stent Master for the Burgh; Director of Town Hospital, 7 New Sneddon
[2] 1841 Census: 47 High street
[3] Monument in Woodside Cemetery: painter died 18/3/1883 aged 86 and his wife Isabella Neilson, died 1846

APPENDIX II

Page 83
[1] Dick & McGregor Directory 1840: shawl manufacturers
[2] 1835 Directory: Allan, 6 Moss street
[3] Director for Middle church Hutcheson's Charity School, Orr street; Director Infant school, 12 Lawn street; Representative for south division Sabbath and Weekday evening schools

Page 84
[1] Medical department of the Dispensary and House of Recovery, 11 Bridge street
[2] 1829 Directory: cloth and tea merchant, 244 High street; in 1837 bought 10 shares in the Glasgow, Paisley, Kilmarnock & Ayr Railway for £500
[3] Ordinary Director, Paisley Commercial Banking Company, 4 Smithhills; Manager qualified by subscription of the Dispensary and House of Recovery, 11 Bridge street
[4] Manager qualified by subscription of the Dispensary and House of Recovery, 11 Bridge street; Director Deaf and Dumb Institution; 1829 Directory: manufacturer, house Burns place; 1835 Directory: of J & J Clark
[5] 1841 Census: flesher, 2 Canal street

Page 85
[1] Town Councillor; Director Paisley Coffee Room, 107 High street; Ordinary Director Paisley & Renfrew Railway (est. 1837)
[2] Preses Princes' Journeymen Society (est. 1769) 85 Canal street; monument in Castlehead Churchyard: manufacturer, born 19/8/1829 died 6/9/1891 and Jane Masterton his wife born 26/1/1826 died 25/10/1905
[3] Commissioner of Police for the New Town; Collector for Hammermen's Society (est. 1760)
[4] 1829 and 1835 Directory: Walter, hosier and draper, 261 High street (Cross)

Page 86
[1] Dick & McGregor Directory 1840: muslin manufacturers, house 10 Back Sneddon street
[2] Dick & McGregor Directory 1840: buckram manufacturer, house 33 Oakshaw street
[3] 1841 Census: and son John aged 30

Page 87
[1] Commissioner of Police for the New Town
[2] Dick & McGregor Directory 1840: shawl manufacturer
[3] Commissioner of Police 5th Ward
[4] Deputy Master St. Mirren's Lodge (No.128) (est. 1749), 24 Williamsburgh; monument in Thread Street UP Churchyard: brick manufacturer in Williamsburgh, died 27/11/1848 aged 49
[5] Monument in Woodside Cemetery: died 1/1/1845 aged 42

⁶ Dick & McGregor Directory 1840: shawl manufacturer
⁷ 1841 Census: Orr street
Page 88
¹ 1829 Directory: George, currier, 37 Gordon's lane
² 1829 Directory: leather cutter, 190 High street
³ 1841 Census: Jane, aged 30, Tuscan warehouse
⁴ Bailie; Director Hutcheson's Charity School, Orr street
⁵ Stent Master for the Burgh; monument in Woodside Cemetery: died 7/7/1846 aged 49
⁶ Manager qualified by subscription of the Dispensary and House of Recovery, 11 Bridge street; Protestant Director Roman Catholic school, Orr street
⁷ Collector Bakers' Society (est. 1777)
⁸ 1841 Census: 6 St. James' street
Page 89
¹ 1829 Directory: John, cooper, 88 Moss street; 1835 Directory, 9 Moss street
² Dick & McGregor Directory 1840: shawl manufacturers
Page 90
¹ 1841 Census: and James aged 30 silk dyer
² Commissioner of Police 5th Ward and Treasurer; Ordinary Director Paisley Water Company (est. 1834); 1829 Directory: manufacturer and dyer, 6 Bridge street; 1835 Directory: [imitation] angola (corruption of angora) manufacturer 59 High street. See *The Paisley Pattern*, Valerie Reilly, 1987 p.34)
³ 1841 Census: with wife Jane aged 35, 25 Moss street
Page 91
¹ 1841 Census: Alexander, aged 40
² 1829 Directory: silk and cotton yarn warehouse 20 Causeyside house 81 Causeyside; Dick & McGregor Directory 1840: late silk merchant
³ 1829 Directory: cashier Paisley Bank, house 2 Bank street; Manager qualified by subscription of the Dispensary and House of Recovery, 11 Bridge street
⁴ 1841 Census: with 25 workforce
Page 92
¹ 1829 and 1835 Directory: manufacturer, 14 Causeyside and Stevenson street
² Director Deaf and Dumb Institution; Dick & McGregor Directory 1840: silk gauze manufacturer
³ 1835 Directory: bleacher and shawl washer, Millerston field
⁴ Dick & McGregor Directory 1840: shawl shop 89 High street
⁵ 1835 Directory: thibet cutter and bleacher, Greenlaw bleachfield
⁶ Monument in Woodside Cemetery: Grocer, Ferguslie – died 1844

Appendix II

Page 93
[1] Treasurer Paisley Young Men's Sabbath Morning Association (est. 1833), 40 George street; Treasurer, Journeymen Tailors' Benevolent Funeral Society (est. 1835), Crossflat
[2] 1829 Directory: keeper Blackhall and Stonefield toll bar; 1835 Directory: grocer and spirit dealer, 8 Neilston road

Page 94
[1] 1829 Directory: Thomas, senior, 217 High street
[2] Medical Referee, Scottish Amicable Life Assurance and Endowment Society; Director Deaf and Dumb Institution; Extraordinary Director Paisley Gas Light Company (est. 1823); monument in Woodside Cemetery: died 15/3/1849
[3] Officer Paisley Funeral Society (est. 1824), 8 Barr street; 1841 Census: with wife Sarah aged 35 living at 45 George street
[4] 1841 Census: Isabella, flesher
[5] Extraordinary Director Paisley Gas Light Company (est. 1823)

Page 95
[1] 1841 Census: victualler, 9 St. James' place

INDEX TO ALEXANDER BORLAND'S ANNOTATIONS

This index covers only the annotations made to Borland's copy of Fowler. The page numbers given are those of the original, and not of this volume. It commences with entries for Paisley, with the remainder of the world at the end. A superscript numeral after the page number indicates the number of times the name appears on that page.

	Page
Accommodation	xiii, 14, 16, 32, 55, 88[2], 91
Baird & Wallace	18
Baking Association	39
Barclay, Andrew	14
Barclay & Pollock	73
Barr & Wallace	87
Barshaw House	68
Bickett & Linn	19
'Black Jock'	35
Blair, Mrs	68
Bligh, James, Junior, & Co	27
Borland, Alexander ('the writer')	27, 42, 70, 74 and note, 90[2], 91
Brand, William	68
Brothel	67
Brough & Sharp	67
Brown & Polson	74
Buchanan, E B	63, 79
Bugle Hall	14
Caldwell & Crawford	30
Calside House	57
Carlile, William, & Co	42
Cartvale House	43
Cessio bonorum	xvi, 31
Chartism, Chartists	25, 36, 71
Che(a)p, James	63
Climie, Mrs	72

Cloth Clubs	54
Coats & Shaw	79
Cochran, Mrs	27
Collinslee	13
Colquhoun, John	22
Cooks	87
Dick, Walter, & Son	33, 61, 77, 79
'Dirty Whyte'	92
'Duke Wellington'	84
Duncan	78
Dunlop	79
Earl Grey, Steamship	92
Egypt Park	21
Ferguslie	34
'Fly'	40
Forrest, William	48
Forrest & Hutton	48
Fullarton, Alexander	88
Fulton, James	77
William, & Sons	70
Galloway, William	17, 78
Galloway & Walker	89
Gallowhill	80
Gardner	26
Gentles, John	54
Gilmour, Thomas	85
Gilmour Street	61
Glasgow Union Bank	36, 76
Good Fellows Society	46, 90
Hamilton, Mrs	39
Hannah	90
Harvey, Brand & Co	16, 18, 31, 58
Hastie, Archibald, MP	21, 22
Hay, Robert	14, 71
Henderson, A P	44, 75
Holms & Andrews	21, 29, 46, 53, 86
Horse trotting	28
Hutton, John	36

Keir, Adam	28
Kerr	77
John	52
King	79
James	85
Mr	15
Thomas	85
William	13
Knox	88
Laird	87
Leckie, Archibald	90
Lochhead, widow	58
Loudon, James	92
Lyall, George	46
Mcalister, William	24, 42
McAlpine & Watson	35
McFarlane	34
James, & Co	63, 66
McGibbon	31
McGilveray & Fleming	36
McKay, Mrs	13
McKerrell & Morgan	30
McLauchland, J.	95
McLean & Dobie	32
McPherson, Caldwell & Gibb	39
Mair, John, & Co	32
Memoirs of Milford	27
Menzies, Graham	84
Millar, Andrew	91
John	18
Millar, John, & Sons	58
Miller	53
Muir	91
James, Senior	87
Murdoch, P	40
Neilson, John	14, 71
Nethercommon	38, 39
Nielson, John, of Nethercommon	38, 39

Non-Intrusionists	69
'Old Schoolmaster'	91
Orr & Wallace	89
Paisley Advertiser	44, 70
Paisley Bank	41, 54
Paisley Commercial Bank	21, 62, 76
Paisley Union Bank	41, 45, 76, 79
Paisley Water Company	50
Paterson	26
Paton, Alex	72
Pattison, Robert	85
Philips, William	71
Pollock & Gilmour	88
Polson, John	22
Porter, James	93
Pretender, the	84
'Proddy Yuill'	95
'Pudding Will'	27
Putter, Leaper and Fencer	46
Ranfurly	82
Reid, Robert	38
Reid & Hanna	88
Robertson, Alexander	93
Saracens Head	36, 37
Savings Bank	45
Semple & Murray	61
Sharp, Thomas	22
William	22
Shawl trade	
Introduction	19, 30, 58
Crisis	35
Muslin	94
Supply to England	80
Simpson & Martin	56
Smith, David	58
Spiers, Baillie	36
'Split The Pea'	72
Stewart, Archibald	57

Index to Alexander Borland's Annotations

Stirrat, James	72
Symington, William	55
Thom, Robert	67
Thomson, Hugh	55
Miss	69
Thomson, Bickett & Co	19
Volunteers	36, 50, 57
Walker, David	60
Watson	35
D	36
'Wee Peerie'	44
Weir, widow	68
Western Bank	18, 20, 41, 42, 51, 56, 60, 63, 71, 76, 79
White, Dr	72
Whitehill, A	35
Willie Dinn, as honest as	34
Wilson & Ballantyne	17
Wingate, Son & Co	36, 89

America	17, 38, 41, 45, 56, 74, 79, 83, 84
New York	87, 90
Australia	90
Ayrshire	
Cessnock Iron Works	64
Kilbirnie	81
Largs	36
Canada	20
Edinburgh	44
England	80
Liverpool	47, 82
London	23, 42, 49, 88
Germany	
Hamburg	61
Glasgow	18, 19, 35, 41, 44, 61, 63, 65, 71, 87, 93, 95
Apothecary Hall	44
Broomielaw	60
Drummond & Kevan	33

Glasgow Evening Post	45
Skaterigg Iron	17
Glasgow, Paisley & Greenock Railway	84
Glasgow, Paisley & Johnstone Canal	39
India	23
Ireland	
Cork	65, 79
Kinross-Shire	21
Kirkcudbrightshire	
Castle Douglas	91
Portugal	
Lisbon	56
Renfrewshire	
Fancy Farm	30
Greenock	15, 33, 55
Househill Iron Co	25
Johnstone	26, 83
Kilbarchan	14, 50, 75
Renfrew	20, 80
South America	28, 42
Cochran, Robert, & Sons	28
Peruvian Bonds	38
Spain	33

PLAN
OF
Paisley
and its
ENVIRONS
FROM AN ACTUAL SURVEY BY
JAMES KNOX
REVISED AND CORRECTED TO THE PRESENT TIME BY
GEO. MARTIN
1839